What people are saying about …

TIGHTROPES AND TEETER-TOTTERS

"Lisa Pennington admits it. This book contains no one-size-fits-all formula for balancing our lives. Thank goodness! Instead, *Tightropes and Teeter-Totters* offers a variety of tools that can be tailored to each reader's unique circumstance. With her usual wit and humor, Lisa's greatest achievement is to speak to our hearts, offering hope that only God can bring for a kind of balance in life's hardest moments."

Amber Lia, bestselling author of *Triggers: Exchanging Parents' Angry Reactions for Gentle Biblical Responses* and blogger at MotherOfKnights.com

"Very few women know what true balance in life really looks like, and even fewer know what healthy self-care is really all about. In *Tightropes and Teeter-Totters*, Lisa gets to the very core of this struggle and paints for us a picture of what it could look like if our hearts were to beat in perfect harmony with that of our heavenly Father. We all must learn how to be good stewards of the greatest resource we have to offer: ourselves. And this book is the perfect place to start!"

Vanessa Hunt, author of *Life in Season*

"In our culture of extremes that makes us constantly wonder if we're doing it wrong, *Tightropes and Teeter-Totters* is a breath of fresh air. Lisa Pennington addresses every crucial area of a woman's life with a thoughtful balance of grace and truth. For every woman on a path to find her place in the center(ish) of God's will, this is a guidebook for the journey."

Jess Wolstenholm, author of the *Pregnancy* and *Baby Companion* books, and creator of Grace for Moms and GatherAndGrow.com

"Lisa Pennington has done it again! Her humor, honesty, and transparency make this book a must read! Her heartfelt suggestions and practical applications will certainly help us all find balance amid 'comedies and tragedies, highs and lows' as we struggle to find proper footing in our lifelong love story written by God."

Roxanne Parks, founder of Winter Summit Ministries, Inc., and author of *Are You Enough?*

TIGHTROPES and TEETER-TOTTERS

TIGHTROPES *and*
TEETER-TOTTERS

FINDING BALANCE IN THE
UPS AND DOWNS OF LIFE

LISA PENNINGTON

David C Cook®

transforming lives together

TIGHTROPES AND TEETER-TOTTERS
Published by David C Cook
4050 Lee Vance Drive
Colorado Springs, CO 80918 U.S.A.

David C Cook U.K., Kingsway Communications
Eastbourne, East Sussex BN23 6NT, England

The graphic circle C logo is a registered trademark of David C Cook.

The website addresses recommended throughout this book are offered as a
resource to you. These websites are not intended in any way to be or imply an
endorsement on the part of David C Cook, nor do we vouch for their content.

LCCN 2016952710
ISBN 978-0-7814-1293-3
eISBN 978-1-4347-1106-9

© 2017 The Anchor Group
Published in association with the literacy agency of D.C. Jacobson &
Associates LLC, an Author Management Company. www.dcjacobson.com.

The Team: Alice Crider, Nicci Hubert, Nick Lee, Jack Campbell, Susan Murdock
Cover Photo: Patience Pennington, thebrightnessproject.com

Printed in the United States of America
First Edition 2017

1 2 3 4 5 6 7 8 9 10

112116

To my husband, James.
Your common sense perfectly balances my
spontaneity. Thanks for putting up with long days
and crazy ideas and changing my mind. I don't
know how you do it, but I'll be forever grateful.

CONTENTS

INTRODUCTION

It's my kinda-sorta dream to be a contestant on *The Amazing Race*. I say "kinda-sorta" because I really just want to travel around the world for free with the option of getting a million dollars at the end. I don't actually want to sleep on the streets or eat bugs.

It's also been my kinda-sorta dream to write a book someday. I have always, since I can remember, felt that calling. The topic changed over the years. When I was thirteen years old, my first idea was that I would write about what it would be like to be married to Donny Osmond and have lots of kids. I mean, the Osmonds had nine children—good golly miss molly! Who *does* that?!

Later on I mostly thought I would write romance novels because I tended to see the world as one long love story. Now as a grown woman with, yes, nine kids of my own, I see it absolutely is a love story! It is a love story between me and God. Or you and God. His love for us is so much better than any Harlequin, and the story needs to be told over and over.

That's my passion, what I love to do more than anything, including eating chocolate. Yes, it's that huge. I am crazy about telling everyone who will listen (or read) about this love story of mine, one that changes all of us. I am driven to shout from the rooftop, "He loves you!"

You are a part of this beautiful love story! You are an amazing woman who is so beautiful I can hardly stand thinking about it right now. I don't care if you're in sweatpants or an Oscar-worthy gown, you are strikingly gorgeous. And God thinks it even more than I do. He sees you.

So I started writing my story, of a loving God who adores me in ways I couldn't have predicted. I see His love not only through my husband and children but also in my home, my friends, even my fifteen-passenger van. That enormous hunk of gas-guzzling metal gets my whole family where we need to go; it's pretty amazing. God's love is in everything we touch, and I had to write it down and share it. After I wrote my first book, *Mama Needs a Do-Over*, I got to hear from women who were in the thick of the hard times in their lives. What a blessing to be a part of someone else's victory! When it came to my next book (this one!), I knew I had to write about finding balance. This love story between God and us is filled with comedies and tragedies, highs and lows, and we need to know how to stay standing.

This love message about balance and joy and hanging on is the result. Everyone I know at some point or another has fallen off track in some way and struggled to find proper footing again. It's happened to me too, many times. So I started asking God, "How do we find balance? Or what does it even look like?"

And then my life got really hard. One of my daughters decided to walk away from our family, and for a time she had no contact with us. And if that wasn't painful enough, people took sides. They started calling me names and believed lies about me; it got pretty ugly. In truth, I wasn't sure how to recover from this. It was just too hard.

Then I remembered my cry to God. It was as though He said to me, "You asked Me how to find balance, so I am showing you."

Oh, well, then I clearly should have chosen a subject such as naps, or snacks.

Many of you have been hurt like this. Divorce, that's gotta rip you up. Any kind of rejection from someone you love. You can get off track in many ways, which is why I have divided this book into nine main areas of a woman's life. Following our first two chapters that examine the meaning of balance, chapter 3, "Me, Myself, and I," will go into the very personal part of life, areas only we can control. Then I'll move into marriage and motherhood: two very vulnerable areas of life. Afterward we will talk about home, ministry and work, friendships, money, taming the tongue, and moods—ouch! Before our conclusion, I've provided a miscellaneous chapter, because women are nothing if not complicated. You will find yourself in each section even if you aren't struggling with that particular area right now. I wanted it to be something you could easily go back to and reread in the future if you hit a bump in one of these roads.

And while the relationship with our daughter remains strained as of this writing, I have found balance with this difficult thing. It's a place where I never wanted to be and I hope you never have to go, but it's really beautiful here. I discovered that my love story was still beautiful and my worth was still high and He loved me even more and all I had to do was trust Him. I found joy and true love and deep truth in the hard times. I found out what you should grab on to when you think you are going to fall. I learned so much more than I knew before. Even though my problem on the outside hasn't changed as much as I would like, on the inside I've found a depth of joy that I never knew before. I hope God will use my struggles to bless you.

I think God wants us to just let go of our tight notions of perfection and grownupping and enjoy ourselves. So I decided to start each chapter with a fun story about times I have gotten off balance. It's a little like looking into my medicine cabinet—you can see what I am up to behind the pages. We have to start there, where the love story begins, with our weaknesses. And believe me, everyone has them; most just don't tell you about them.

Whatever small or big challenge you are facing, we are here together to help you figure out how to find balance while you're being pulled closer to God. When I found my way to complete joy again after my very hard situation, I discovered I had more choices than I thought. I wasn't completely at the mercy of my circumstance, and neither are you.

My dream for you is that at the end of this book, in addition to having some new tools for dealing with your struggle, you feel permission to let go of ideas you have that aren't helping your life and grab on tight to the love story you are living. I hope you will see yourself as a beautiful woman of possibilities and ready to pull yourself up from whatever you're dealing with.

And don't forget how your love story ends: happily ever after.

BALANCE: WHAT IS IT?

A false balance is an abomination to the LORD,
but a just weight is his delight.

Proverbs 11:1

I always loved the playground when I was a kid. That sandy-colored packed dirt on the ground and kids who were willing to play with one another even if they had never met before. Of course, this was in the '70s when all playground equipment was made of metal and there were no child safety laws in place. I'm surprised more of us didn't die from scrapes filled with rust and metal shavings.

The teeter-totter (aka, seesaw) was a favorite of my brother's and mine. We would take our places on the ends of the board and start pushing off with our legs, trying to hit the ground as hard as we could in an effort to make the other one fall off. It didn't matter that when we hit, it jarred our backs and hurt our behinds. No amount of personal pain could distract from the fun of the *whack* that jostled the opposite person to a near fall (I am starting to understand why I now need to see my chiropractor so often). Plus, we knew the payoff would come seconds later when it was our turn to go flying upward and hang on for dear life.

On the days my brother wasn't there to totter with me, I liked to stand in the center of the seesaw and try to balance. I would take a wide stance with a foot on either side of center and see if

I could make the board level. This was particularly appealing to me because it felt like something I could master. It was a simple, personal, yet deeply important challenge. Just me and that long board working together to accomplish something that, in my seven-year-old mind, no one else in the whole wide world had ever been able to do: achieve perfect balance.

I haven't been on a playground teeter-totter for many years now, but the image flashes into my mind frequently as I go through my life. The ups and downs; sometimes in life I am alone, sometimes with a friend. Occasionally there is someone on the other end who is not-so-playfully trying to knock me off. I go up, I go down, and in the end my behind hurts, but I still want to do it again tomorrow.

If only balance in life were as simple to achieve as in a childhood game.

ABOUT FALLING

What is funny is that while I am not writing this book to talk about physical balance, I do have a tendency to fall over. I don't know what causes it; I don't get dizzy or have any warning. I just topple. When I see children fall, which they do on a daily basis, they just pop back up and keep running. But at my age, if I fall, it is two weeks of limping plus an extra ten days of complaining before I am moving at full speed again.

Falling is part of life. Maybe it's more a part of mine than it is yours, but we all fall down and have to find ways to steady ourselves occasionally. We can try to be graceful, but it really doesn't work. The grace comes in when you are finding ways to recover. It's in laughing at yourself, forgiving yourself and other people, dusting yourself off, and trying again. The example you set for others isn't in the fact that you fell, but in how you joyfully recovered and kept going.

In her book *Bittersweet*, Shauna Niequist talked about recovering from a hard time like this: "It's easy to want to give up under the weight of what we're carrying. It seems sometimes like the only possible choice. But there's always, always another choice, and transformation is waiting for us just beyond that choice."[1]

NONPHYSICAL BALANCE

Fortunately, this book is about balance in other areas of life, such as marriage, motherhood, and money. These are also places where I fall occasionally, but I have found ways to get back up and keep moving, make improvements, and do better the next time. I don't have to pretend to be okay because I know that everyone messes up or gets hit with unexpected problems. I know where to turn to get back on my feet, and I want to share that with you.

Falling, getting up, trying again, over and over, is how we learn. We can't come out of the womb knowing how to balance a bank account or be a good friend. We learn over time from our mess-ups and mistakes. When we were babies, we learned to walk because our bodies and minds taught us how to lean slightly left when we started to fall right, and eventually it became instinctive. Then we moved on to the next challenge and so on until we were adults. But the learning didn't stop when we hit eighteen. I know I have changed a lot in my adult years, far beyond learning how to walk. I learned how to handle broken relationships and how to control my spending and where to let go in my mothering when I felt like hanging on. I have learned to deal with emotional breakdowns and to take care of a home that sometimes seems like it is falling apart. I am constantly changing and finding better balance.

WHAT BALANCE IS *NOT*

Before I talk more about what balance is, I want to share some things that we are not trying to achieve.

IT IS NOT ABOUT PERFECTION

We get this idea in our heads that if we are perfectly balanced then our lives are perfect. But that isn't possible no matter how many good choices we make or how hard we try. Perfection is a product of our imagination and watching too many Disney movies.

Being a princess with a castle and beautiful flowing hair is not my life, and I am guessing it's not yours either. And I definitely don't have magic potions to help me. Ain't no fairy godmother gonna swoop in and give me until midnight to make my dreams come true. Nope, I have to work it, sister.

I urge you to also let go of the idea that anyone else's life is perfect. Disney princesses and hair commercials aren't real, and movie stars have problems. In case you haven't seen any reality TV lately, famous people are more of a mess than we are most of the time. I promise you that no celebrity is always happy, always clean, always confident. They can't be—just look at what people say about them in the magazines at the newsstands. It can't be easy to read what the tabloids have to say about you and hear lies that people believe because they think they know you from seeing you in a movie. Friends, celebrities have the least "perfect" lives of all.

God tells us not to compare ourselves to others. All it does is feed lies to us for no reason!

Galatians 6:4 says, "But let each one test his own work, and then his reason to boast will be in himself alone and not in his neighbor."

Perfection is a joy stealer! We are going to shake off that idea and just be ourselves. You find your own level of balance and I will find mine and we can both be doing great. It's a good thing to be different; otherwise, God would have just made a bunch of robots.

IT'S NOT ABOUT CONTROL

If you spend your life trying to control every area in your world and, let's face it, trying to control other people, you'll be miserable. Self-control is good; life control is bad. As a reformed control freak, I can testify that letting go of your desire to have your own way is a blessing to everyone around you.

Webster's 1828 dictionary says to control is "to overpower; to subject to authority; to counteract; to have under command."

That is weighty! If you really look at what you are trying to control, you may discover that it is not something you have authority over in the first place. And to overpower? Man, that's just exhausting.

I don't want that. It says to God, "I don't need You." It minimizes my life to only what I can do for myself, when God is ready to give us so much more than that. I have news for you: you're not always right. We have to accept that in order to stop trying to be in charge of everything. Believe me, I find myself trying to grab those reins back too often, and I have learned to stop myself and see how exhausting and unnecessary it is.

John Maxwell, a man I greatly admire, wrote about this so beautifully in his book *Learning from the Giants*: "Too often we are like a horse who allows his master to put a bit in his mouth, but then fights against it. What we don't seem to understand is that if we allow God to have complete control of the reins in our life, He will stay with us continually, and He will guide us away from the danger, see that we are fed, and lead us back home—the very things Jacob longed for."[2]

I love analogies. My simple mind can understand them so much better than straight talk. I'm pretty sure God put all those parables in the Bible just for me; otherwise, I would not understand much of it on my own.

IT'S NOT ABOUT STAYING IN THE MIDDLE

No one wants a life of mediocrity—that would be boring! We learn from the lows and we expand in the highs, and we need those times to build a mature, experienced life.

The woman who stays in the middle can never grow into that wise, older woman God talked about in Titus 2. You need to mess up, you need to have suffering, you need those extreme highs to know what to reach for. I have read the entire Bible and I can't find anything in it that I would consider "middle ground." It is mostly suffering and trials mixed with the most triumphant victories in the history of the world.

Our comfy lives with remote controls and air-conditioning have lulled us into thinking that there is a zone we need to stay in to be happy. But it isn't true! The only zone of true joy is wherever God has placed us. The balance is there, my friends, not in our Americanized comfort.

LASTLY, IT'S NOT ABOUT A FORMULA THAT WORKS FOR EVERYONE

Not only are you and I different from each other, but the people in our lives are different, which makes an infinite number of possible problems and solutions. Yes, there are principles we can all follow, but the way it looks on you will be different than how it looks on me.

Not only does this eliminate pressure to try to live your life by someone else's decisions, but it also removes the need to judge how other people choose to find their balance. Don't misunderstand; I am not talking about sin or godliness. This is much different than that. This is about which direction you decide to take to reach the godly outcome you desire.

My husband and I are so opposite that we take a different route to almost every destination. When we pull out of the driveway to go to the grocery store, I turn left and he turns right, depending on who is driving. I'm not kidding. We have different goals for our travel. I like the scenic, pleasant route, and he likes the direct, boring, and lifeless path. Not that I'm judging him. The bottom line is that we both end up at the store at pretty much the same time and we get the shopping done (although don't get me started on how opposite our shopping strategies are!). There is no wrong route to the store, and generally there isn't a right or wrong way to find balance. Just stick with the principles I am going to give you and you'll find a beautiful, unique, joy-filled path!

SO WHAT *IS* BALANCE?

Balance is quickly figuring out how hard to lean into the unexpected gust of wind so you don't blow away. Sometimes we start to fall from being knocked over, even on purpose. There are ways to brace yourself. Lies, for example, can knock me down and make me want to go back to bed with my head covered for a week. But if I grab on to the truth and hang on, I can stay upright, then move on. The amazing thing about this is that we are frankly better off, wiser, and stronger for next time!

Balance is the result of an intentional reaction to an extreme situation. We are not slaves to our emotions and attitudes. We can actually be large and in charge of both our external responses *and* our internal responses.

Balance is looking at areas in your life that are not working and finding measurable, specific actions to change them. It's one thing to decide to make changes, but if we don't have a plan in place and ways to know if what we are doing is working, then it doesn't work. Oh, it might help, but a measurable plan makes it *so much* better! I'm going to help you find easy, practical ways to do that. Believe in yourself. I believe in you!

You're looking at your life right now and can likely pinpoint areas that you want to change. Maybe you are too emotional. Or perhaps you're feeling like a failure as a mom, but your finances are doing pretty well and you have found balance in your service to the community. It's a mix. The areas of a woman's life that I am going to cover can each send us into orbit at times in our lives and make us desperate to feel secure again. Then when we get one thing pretty manageable, another issue pops up somewhere else.

That's good. That is where you are supposed to be! Having nine children, I often say that there are always two kids who are causing me to really dig in and figure out how to help them and occasionally a third who is dealing with some less acute problems. But it has never been all nine at once. I consider that a gift from God. And by the way, it is not the same two each time. It varies, as if they are taking turns. Oh sure, a few of them seem to be on the high-need list more often than their siblings, but even my hardest kid isn't always causing the struggle.

It's the same with these areas of life. Most of you will be struggling with only two to three of these areas at a time. But eventually your life will hit a bump in each of them. Even if you're not a mom or if you don't have kids at home anymore, you will have kids to deal with—be it grandchildren or nieces and nephews or kids at church—and need to find ways to balance that for yourself. If you don't own your home, you still have a space to manage and will have to figure out how to handle the ideas between what you want and what is actually available to you.

2

SPELLING IT OUT

Beloved, I pray that all may go well with you and that you
may be in good health, as it goes well with your soul.

3 John 1:2

I tend to forget things, such as where I put my reading glasses or how to delete an app on my phone. I once found a pair of scissors in the fridge that I had been searching for.

One morning I was running late and couldn't find my car keys. This was unusual because my car is "keyless," so I don't have to ever take them out of my purse. This new invention, by the way, has changed my life. I have a keyless lock on my front door as well and don't have to carry house keys, because in the past I have been locked out a few times.

So on this morning I plopped into the front seat of my car and urged the kids to hurry and get buckled because we were late for an orthodontist appointment. But when I pushed the start button on the car, a message popped up on the dashboard that said, "Key Not Detected."

"That's *impossible*!" I muttered to myself as I rummaged through my purse for the fob. Dig, dig, dig, pull out some stray receipts, old Kleenex, an earring I had been looking for, no key fob. I sat back and tried to wake up the part of my brain that held random information and remember if I had done something with my keys. But the only thing that popped into my head was panic of being late to the ortho, which meant getting the evil eye from the receptionist—something I wanted to avoid at any cost.

I ran back in the house and started flinging things around my bedroom in search of the keys. I talked to myself, saying things like, "This can't be my fault. I never take them out of my purse!" I texted my husband and asked him if he knew where my car key was. He had no idea.

Just as I was going back to the car for another look, my adult son was coming into the house (he lives in a guesthouse on our property) and I murmured something as I blew past him about not being able to find my keys.

"Oh!" he said with a tail-between-his-legs look. "I have them. I am *so sorry* I forgot to put them back in your purse." I was frozen with shock. He had never used my car or done anything with it. Why on earth?!

"I wanted to surprise you by washing your car so I snuck the keys from your purse and pulled the car around to the back where the hose is to wash it."

Um, in my rush had I completely missed the fact that my car had been washed?

He continued, "But before I got around to washing it, I had to do something else, so Dad told me to put the car back where you park it. So I moved it back and kept the keys so I could wash it later. That was yesterday and I guess I forgot about it after that."

I had mixed emotions. Yes, he had caused me to have a near breakdown, tear my bedroom apart, be late for the ortho, and believe I was developing early onset dementia. But on the other hand, his motives were so thoughtful and I really would have loved to have my car washed.

He went back to his place, got my key fob, and brought it to me. In the two minutes I waited, I had a serious talk with myself about not blowing up about the fob. No lecture, no rejection, no guilt trip. I decided to smile, thank him, then shut up.

In the end I did get the receptionist's evil eye, my car was still dirty, and I felt shaken from the wild search. But I decided to be thankful. Thankful that I am not—yet, at least—losing my mind. Thankful that my son tried to do something nice for me even though his method was flawed. And thankful that we can even afford to go to the orthodontist. Or that I have a car at all!

Although you can bet I found a secret spot in my purse to keep my key fob after that.

BALANCE

Every day of our lives is filled with some small situations that knock us off balance. We then get to choose to use those times as lessons and opportunities for growth. In the case of the lost key fob (hey, that sounds like a Nancy Drew mystery!), I had learned from past mistakes what happens when I react badly and dump guilt on my son. It doesn't help anything. So I purposed not to in that moment even though I really wanted to throw the book at him. Even if he had taken the keys for a less touching reason, I didn't have to react harshly.

It helps to have practical tools we can reach for when we are trying to cope with a difficult situation. One thing I use to find balance is a fun acronym. I like acronyms because they help forgetters like me remember the steps.

Begin

Assess

Learn

Account

Notify

Change

Endure

Let's go through them.

B IS FOR BEGIN

Seems obvious, right? But it's not. So many people have ideas and plans but never do anything about them. You have to *start* if you ever want to finish! That means getting my booty out of my recliner and taking some action steps. That means building up my strength and determination to do something about my fall.

Picture the lady in the hospital bed who fell and broke her hip. I use this image because the older I get, the more real this possibility becomes. She lies there, day after day, recovering from her painful fall and surgery. She could just lie there waiting to get better and then start walking. *Or* she could look for ways to get going. If she can only do small exercises, then do that. She can make herself sit up a little longer each day. She can watch for opportunities to use her time in bed as a help to someone else, which in turn will keep her spirits up. If she does any of those things, she will not only recover more quickly but also be a beacon of hope for others.

When you realize you're off balance, begin to move in a way that will change it. Finding balance is a lifelong effort, so I am doing this right along with you. Let's get up and get going. Let's start today by working toward staying upright in our struggles.

A IS FOR ASSESS

Once we know we are out of balance in an area and are ready to begin, we have to stop to figure out why. Oh, we can moan about the injustice or how hard things are, but that doesn't help. Even if there is an injustice, you can find balance anyway. We don't like to look at ourselves honestly; it can be kind of scary. What if we discover that we are a hot mess? My friend, I can guarantee that already, so let's just stop pretending. You need to work on some areas of your life. You just do. Everyone does! Accepting your flaws is the best way to start to fix any problem. Maybe you can't even change them! Maybe you need to find ways to work with your weak areas.

For example, I tend to be distant when I meet new people. I am introverted and generally uncomfortable. I thought I should work on being more outgoing, but try as I might, I couldn't do it. I would forget people's names, and occasionally I would forget that I had already met them. It's something I would like to change about myself, but that doesn't seem to be working! So upon evaluation I realized that I would be wiser to spend my efforts improving other areas of my life and concentrate on my strengths. For me that's teaching and edification. I learned to tell people, "I care about you, but I may forget your name even though it's important to me!" I surrounded myself with friends who are great at remembering names and making people feel welcome. Those changes made a huge difference in my ministry and improved people's impression of me. I am open about knowing my weaknesses and asking forgiveness where I flub up. Sometimes the solution is to let an idea go.

Step back and look at your situation. Narrow it down into small chunks and identify a few parts that you can work on. If it's finances, you can have a big goal like being debt-free; but then break it into smaller goals, such as "I want to pay off that one credit card by the end of the year." You can break it down even further by planning to skip that fancy coffee every morning and add five dollars to the credit-card-payoff fund. Very doable. You know what you want.

If you want a broken friendship restored, that may not be possible. But there are things you can do to find balance in that situation. You can accept your friend, forgive her, be willing to lovingly move on, and find freedom from the pain. Break disappointment into smaller bits and see it for what it is. You learn, you grow, you recover, you move on.

When you're thrown a curve, take a second to identify what is the best way to respond to accomplish what you want. Your goals in life are unique and your reactions should be also. Sometimes you duck, sometimes you swing, sometimes you chase the ball—it's specific to you. (My apologies if that sports analogy doesn't make sense; sports is my weakest area of expertise.)

Kristen Strong, in her book *Girl Meets Change*, provided another way to say this:

> Of course it's perfectly okay to ask the questions. But when we are asking questions from change, we sometimes need to change the questions we ask. It's not about "Why is this happening to me?" but "What is God trying to teach me?" and "What does God want me to accomplish during this change?" Asking the right questions provides learning opportunities that help us uncover what God is teaching us as well as what God is doing through us.[1]

L IS FOR LEARN

We should always, always be learning! Read books, go to seminars, find wise people and ask questions, study, grow, expand our knowledge. And the number one way to grow is to read the Bible as often as possible.

There is no better way to know how to right any fall than knowing God's Word. I can't stress this enough. No, really, if I could get your highlighter out of your drawer for you right now and circle this section, I would.

This is the biggest, most valuable suggestion I have for you in knowing how to react in a pressure situation: read your Bible every day, even if you have only five minutes. You can get a Bible app and read just a few verses. Or search words like *peace* or *fear* and see for yourself what the Bible has to say about certain aspects of life. More times than I can count I've had an idea about how I should respond to something, but when I checked my Bible, it had other principles that showed me my idea was bad. I was drawing from my feelings of "right and wrong," but when I really look, I see that it says I have been off base just enough to give a damaging response and get myself into more trouble. Reacting in a stressful situation without making sure you know what the Bible says can lead to a much bigger mess than what you started with.

I am including prayer and praise in this principle. Reading the Bible is great, but prayer and praise bring it to life! Talk directly to God, tell Him your fears and struggles, and let Him pour wisdom into you through the Holy Spirit. Prayer takes the knowledge of Scripture from your head and draws it into your heart. It becomes your source of comfort and new ideas! Praise takes that to a new level of enthusiasm for who God is and what He does. Be informed, be thankful, be humble, be renewed.

A (#2) IS FOR ACCOUNT

We have to have a way to know if our responses are getting us to our goals. In each area that you are going to work on, you need some way to measure how "off" you are and how effective your changes are. They may not be immediate, but you should see at least small signs that what you are doing is helping.

This is not always easy and will be different in each section. In the money section it's easy to measure. Either you're getting slowly out of debt or you aren't. If you're trying to lose weight, you can measure pounds. But in friendships or motherhood not only is it hard to measure, but the problems change as you make personal changes. Other people are involved with their own sets of issues and knowing whether what you are doing is working may be harder. But I am not going to leave you hanging. We will talk about ways to measure relationship problems and other difficult-to-determine factors.

According to Webster's 1828 dictionary, the word *measure* means "that by which extent or dimension is ascertained, either length, breadth, thickness, capacity, or amount."

Without a way to determine the dimension, how do you know if you have righted your imbalance? One thing to do is to be sure that your goals are measurable. You want your husband to be happy; that's not a measurable goal. He won't be happy all the time, and his happiness is dependent on uncontrollable circumstances. Instead, when you are thinking of a goal to set, figure out what makes him happy and what is causing his misery, then create a goal to eliminate the misery causes and add in more of his pleasures. Did we go fishing more? Yes. Measurable success. Did I hug him every day when he got home from work? Yes. That is measurable. If it didn't help him find more happiness, try something else.

Think about length, breadth, thickness, capacity, and amount when you are determining how to measure if something is working. Inches, minutes, gallons (liters if you live outside the US), pounds, ounces, weeks, decibels, speed, dollars, degrees, milligrams, watts, amps, and I am not even going into the hundreds of measurements I wouldn't understand if I tried.

I will spend time in each chapter working on measurability. It's not as hard as you think. :)

N IS FOR NOTIFY

Notify someone else of your plans and goals. You are not on your own, even if you feel like it. Often I find that my refusal to share my problems with others is what keeps me from changing because no one is holding me accountable. I like to believe I can do this on my own, but it doesn't really work.

Several blessings come with accountability. First, someone is holding you to your goals and will motivate you to keep going. Knowing that someone is watching and caring does wonders for your resolve to stick with it when you're struggling.

But another benefit of telling other people what your goals are is it forces you to admit that you make mistakes. You can't ask for help if you have no problems, and if you're really going to change, you have to declare your own difficulty and not just blame someone else. Even if your issue is with another person, you can ask someone close to you to hold you accountable by telling them what your personal goals are (responding with love, being kind, and so forth) and asking them to help you and pray for you.

Share your vision for the situation with someone wise in that area, tell them how you are measuring the outcome, and ask them to check on you from time to time. Let them know you are looking for truth and not sugarcoated advice. If they see you getting off kilter, you want to know. If you fail to do the things you have determined to do, you want them to feel free to reprimand you gently.

Your spouse is the most obvious person to do this. They know you better than anyone. A trusted friend, pastor, counselor, or even an online friend who you trust can be someone you ask to hold you accountable. This shows them a level of trust that can also build up their confidence and allow them to grow closer to God in the process.

Accountability makes a *huge* difference!

C IS FOR CHANGE

At some point we have to act on our newfound discovery of all of these things. You can't just look at your solution; you have to grab it. The idea itself won't keep you from falling further.

In order to keep from just sitting on the ground at your end of the teeter-totter, you have to push yourself up with your legs. The fun in life is in the ups and the lessons in life are in the downs, but we have to actually move and react in order to have both. Sure, we could just sit there, never moving. It feels safe. But it's not legitimately safe because something could still come along and knock us off. And wouldn't it be sad if we didn't get to experience that feeling of flying before falling off?

Believe me, some days I wake up wishing I could just stay in bed and not face what's ahead of me. The temptation to avoid problems and just sleep can seem so lovely. But then I realize that I will also miss the sweet moments, such as laughing with my kids and being their mom and even cleaning my house, which can give me a sense of satisfaction. I can't just sit on the end of the seesaw with my behind on the ground and enjoy my life. I have to move.

But I added the word *change* intentionally because it's not just movement, but a very purposeful action. Flailing around hoping to find a place to hang on won't work. Instead, we do the other steps first and save this until we have done them. Determine to start, look at the problem, read the Bible and pray, measure, find accountability, and then change.

This last step, though, is the hardest.

E IS FOR ENDURE

Endurance is a "continuance; a state of lasting or duration; continuance without sinking or yielding to the pressure; sufferance; patience," according to Webster's.

Lack of patience is something that can kill your success. We want immediate and complete results or we think our plan isn't working. Sometimes a plan can take years to work. You need to be patient with God, be willing to adjust, and know that it's rarely a quick fix when it comes to righting a mess. Don't lose hope because something is taking time. Time is your friend.

When you feel tempted to quit, look at your goals. Are you getting any closer? Are you feeling pressure from outside sources? Have you lost hope in the process? You don't recover from a surgery in a day, but that doesn't mean the surgery didn't work. You won't get out of debt in a week, but that doesn't mean you should stop trying. You won't drop twenty pounds in a month (unless you're on

The Biggest Loser), but you keep trying. Tweak, alter, shift, evaluate, but don't quit!

Sticking to it is a gift. Patience is a blessing. It's when you have to wait for something that you find out who you truly are. If I could lose weight in an hour, I wouldn't have the character I have developed from the effort of sacrificing my craving for something bigger. Some things change in a month, and others take a lifetime. If your goal is good, then relax and enjoy the process!

John MacArthur said this in his book *Found: God's Peace*: "At the proper time, God will exalt us. Paul used a Greek term that speaks of lifting us out of our present trouble. For the Christian, even the worst trial is only temporary. *Remember that*, for you *will* be tempted to conclude that because there is no end in sight, there is no end at all. Don't believe it for a minute; God promises to lift you out."[2]

HOW TO

These ideas are fine, but let's talk turkey. How does all of this stuff fit into my life? I mean, I got issues. We all do! Every person from the messed-up neighbor down the street to the woman you admire down the row from you at church is dealing with some life struggles and needs to find ways to balance. If you're on a high, you need to brace for the letdown. If you're falling, you need to grab hold of a truth to keep yourself from getting hurt too badly. Let's not hide the imperfections from one another. Our efforts to look like we have no problems are what cause other women to feel inadequate; plus, sometimes we fool even ourselves for a while and don't even try to make changes. I will be the first to stand up right now and shout, "I am a *mess*!" and you can relax. Because I know you're a mess too.

When an issue arises in your life—from a simple mix-up that left an important ingredient off the grocery list to a more extreme loss, such as being betrayed by a friend that you thought you could trust—these steps will help you decide how to react and find your own way of balance.

So let's look at a quick, easy example (we'll dig into the hard stuff in a moment!) using the BALANCE acronym. Here's the situation: Someone used up the last of the butter and you were planning to make cookies. You're angry about this! Let's take our imaginary deep breath and see how BALANCE can help us.

BEGIN: You can go to the store again, call and ask a friend for butter, decide not to make the cookies, use a substitute, bake something different that doesn't call for butter, or you can pout and have a fit and phone your friend to complain about your rotten husband who didn't get the butter even though you reminded him twice. (Kidding about the last one.)

ASSESS: Sometimes you can pretend for a minute that you are a reporter doing a story on this problem. What will the headline be? "Mom Freaks Out over Missing Butter!" or "Making Cake Instead of Cookies Solves Problems." Which one do you want to describe you? I want my headline to be "Woman Figures Out How to Eat Cake *and* Cookies without Gaining Weight." But that's just me.

What is the purpose of the cookies? Are they for a party or for the kids to take to school? Does it have to be that specific recipe? There are so many questions to ask yourself to identify what it is you want. Sometimes getting what you planned, in this case being able to make that recipe right now, is not one of your options.

LEARN: After I have given myself an objective look, I check what the Bible says. If you think it doesn't have anything to say about this, you are mistaken. Maybe it doesn't talk about cookie recipes specifically, but it does have things to say about how we treat others, what our attitude needs to be, putting ourselves last, and so forth. It has wisdom about honoring your husband and raising your children that might come in to play here.

ACCOUNT: Does not having butter warrant the Texas-sized fit we just had? The size of the problem needs to be approximately the same as the size of our reaction. What tends to happen is that we get overwhelmed. The days are long and hard, and sometimes by the time we get around to the cookie baking, we are at the end of our rope and we blow like Old Faithful. It's not just the butter we are exploding about. It is *every single time* we asked our husband to pick up something and he forgot. It is about feeling disrespected and unheard and unloved. But the people around us see us having a fit over butter and don't understand the flow that runs beneath. They wonder what the issue is because to them it looks like not that big of a deal.

Taking the time to measure the problem either by time or size or weight is extremely helpful in the balance process. You need to know how much to add to the other side of the seesaw to get yourself back into the air again. There has to be something down that beam that weighs about the same as you or you won't get your booty off the ground no matter what you do. Measure.

I know we're using a light example; although, in my defense, butter pretty much makes the world go 'round. But butter isn't really our problem here. It's lack of patience, attachment to our own plans, and lack of contentment with what we do have. Do you identify with any of those? Yeah, I do too. I want to stop crashing over things like butter and be a better example to my family and friends. So let's keep going.

NOTIFY: Now that you have checked your attitude and measured the true weight of the problem, it's a good idea to add in some accountability. In this case you might want to ask your husband to hold you accountable. This will sound counterintuitive if you see him as being the one who caused the problem. Well, maybe he is the reason you don't have butter, but he isn't the reason you responded to it with the force of an atomic bomb. That's on you. Think about going to him and apologizing and letting him know that you are sorry you overreacted. Tell him you want to work on this, and ask him to let you know (maybe he should stand back at first since you're both going to have to get used to this new plan) when you might be a teensy bit out of balance in your attitude about it.

Letting him in on your goal of being more balanced in your responses is going to help him see that you know you're part of the problem. You don't get to put any blame on him during the accountability talk. This is just to let him know you're working on responding better. Maybe he will be inspired to change; maybe not. That can't be part of your goal in sharing with him.

CHANGE: Now the intentional action step. This example isn't too hard to figure out. Just smile and change the recipe, or go without, or proceed down whatever path you choose. The smile part is the big challenge. Have you ever noticed how a smile can change your perspective? It is meant to communicate joy and love in any language, and when you do it, even a little forced, you will warm up your heart a little. Like the Grinch and the sound of the Whos singing, your heart can grow a few sizes if you make yourself close your mouth and smile. You can find a place of cheerfulness after you've had a few minutes to get over the problem. Set a goal to not let yourself fuss in your head about it after five minutes. Remember, we aren't going for perfection here! But we do want to learn to move on.

ENDURE: Lastly, have patience with yourself. You will get bent out of shape again. Just keep trying and apologizing and reaching for that future when you easily roll with the butter problems. I am living proof that you do start to get better about these little things after a time of intentionally working on being better balanced. I haven't had a butter fit in at least five years.

I want you to look at your life through the magnifying glass of finding balance and see that it is in the small changes where you will find giant results. A teeny, seemingly insignificant shift in one area can affect all other categories. Altering one part of your response can be like creating ripples in water—they extend out from the point of impact.

Our kids see us have a fit over missing butter and they react by being rude to a friend. We complain to our husband and he carries that attitude to the office. And it spreads from there. Ripples. But the good news is that our changes have the same effect. When we take a breath and joyfully fix a problem, it carries over to our relationships and the people around them.

Finding balance is not a onetime action; it requires repeatedly stepping back and looking at how we react and respond to the things that throw us off. We get better at it, as I did with "The Case of the Lost Key." I responded with grace instead of anger. That wasn't easy, friends; I was supremely irritated during that moment. My reaction was an improvement over previous incidents, and I will hopefully continue to grow in that area.

Now let's embrace the journey of finding balance together.

3

ME, MYSELF, AND I

*Now may the God of peace himself sanctify you completely,
and may your whole spirit and soul and body be kept
blameless at the coming of our Lord Jesus Christ.*

1 Thessalonians 5:23

THE STORY OF THE THREAD

Taking care of yourself and your personal needs is important, even though we moms sometimes convince ourselves we don't need to do so. Personally, I crave alone time, and one day I decided to slip out to our front porch to sneak in a few minutes to myself. At the time we had a newborn baby, a two-year-old, and a three-and-a-half-year-old. Life was definitely, um, full.

I nursed the baby and got her down for a nap and felt the strong urge for some alone time. It had been a normal challenging day with the little ones, and my husband, James, worked a very stressful job that kept him at the office late at night. So I was alone with the kids. all. day. long.

I peeked in on the toddlers, who were playing so sweetly that I decided not to tell them I was going outside. They were fine; plus, I could hear them through the open windows. I really needed a "no one knows where I am" kind of moment. I grabbed myself a cup of tea and slipped out to steal some peace. All was quiet in the house for fifteen minutes as I sat on the front porch just soaking in the sun. Although it was years ago, I can still vividly remember the feeling of leaning my head back and letting the sun warm my face.

I felt so much better after my quiet time, even though it was only fifteen minutes. I felt ready to go back inside and hoped I might get another half hour to do a few chores before the baby woke up and the place came back to life. I pushed myself off the porch and stretched a nice, long, relaxing stretch before heading back through the door. I was a woman ready for anything. Or so I thought.

As I stepped to the doorway, something felt *off*. Not sure what it was, I took another step and looked around, trying to be silent, listening for the kids. I heard nothing. One more step, then *bam*! I tripped over a tangle of thread going across the entryway and fell to the floor. It turned out that my two toddlers, who had apparently learned to communicate like silent ninjas, had created the weirdest mess I ever saw.

They had gotten into my spools of thread, of which I had about a hundred because I did a lot of sewing, and also found several containers of toothpicks (that to this day I have no idea why I had that many toothpicks). Using their newfound toys, these two little darlings created some kind of free art all over the house. Thread was wound around *everything*. Into the thread they had tied toothpicks, which formed a creation even Picasso would have thought was freaky. Twisted formations filled so many places that it was literally impossible to walk or sit in our living room and dining room without stepping on a toothpick or tripping over thread.

My fifteen minutes of sweet sun and silence had cost me two hours of crawling around on the floor searching for toothpicks and trying to untie thread knots from the legs of my dining room chairs. Some of them were impossible to remove and I think they might still be there twenty-two years later. I tried to get the two culprits to help me clean it all up, but apparently a two-year-old is much better at winding thread around a chair than he is at unwinding it. The mess got worse as they tried to undo it, so I was on my own.

Was it worth it? Yes, it was! I was able to feel the sun on my face and have a moment to myself, and then I discovered how incredibly creative my children were! Those toothpick-and-thread babies are now full-grown adults, and I miss those days of innocent fun. And oh yeah, you can be sure I will tell this story at their wedding rehearsals, and to their babies, and to their grandchildren …

YOU ARE WONDERFULLY MADE

This chapter is all about the value of *you*! God has something to say about how special you are:

> 1. He knows every hair on your head. Yep, even those gray ones we pluck out! Every part of you is known to Him, and He loves it all (Luke 12:7).
> 2. You are a new self! Not selfie, no not that. Self. You are made new by His grace, and whatever mess you have been carrying around with you is gone (Eph. 4:24).

> 3. You shine! Knowing Him means you are a shining light to those around you, even when you don't feel it, because it comes from Him and not you alone (2 Cor. 4:6).

Taking care of yourself is the most important thing you can do to find balance in every other area. This isn't the self-centered "me time" that you hear about in the world. This is replenishing, refilling, recovery time. It can look the same because it might involve shopping or going to a movie in the middle of the day or enjoying coffee on the back patio, but it's not about what you are outwardly doing. It's about what you are doing inside. Are you feeding your mind, body, and spirit?

We are all made of those three parts: mind, body, and spirit, and we have to take care of each area in order to succeed in the rest of the sections in this book. Our mothering, marriage, and other areas of our lives won't thrive if we, personally, aren't healthy and managing our own needs. I am talking about what is in our control, such as diet and prayer time. Other things, such as illness and past mistakes, are out of our hands, and for those we must let go and trust the One who knows what is best for us.

God created us with bodies that need rest and food and exercise. He made us with souls that need refreshing and spirits to soar with gratitude toward Him. All of those things are what you and I are made of, and it's high time we realized our own worth and took care of those parts of ourselves.

It's like when the flight attendant tells us to put on our own oxygen masks before helping anyone else. We must go against our instinct and take care of ourselves first! Now, we may have to do it at 5:00 a.m. or trade friends for babysitting or juggle appointments, but we can make room for it in our lives. I remember when I was nursing my babies I would carry the screaming baby, who thought she was starving, into the kitchen to get myself a full glass of cold water. I would straighten my room a bit, put the water on the table by the chair where I nursed, and sit down to take care of her. It took me only two to three minutes to create a relaxing space and make sure I was cared for while I fed her. And the baby was fine, even though she didn't agree. Friend, you are not being selfish by taking care of yourself. You are helping everyone around you by being healthy and as balanced as you can be. In the end, when you stand before the throne of grace, it's just you standing there. You must take care of yourself.

I will tell you some things I do to keep my personal needs in balance, but they may not work for you. I urge you not to get hung up on trying to do what fits me, but to embrace the meaning of it and reinterpret it for yourself.

MIND

Managing the needs of my mind (which I am using synonymously with the word *soul*) is one area of self-care. That will look different for each of us. What I need to have a healthy mind may not be the same thing you need. As an introvert, I especially crave alone time, which as a mom of nine kids isn't so easy to get. Being alone feeds my soul like a banana feeds a monkey. I use monkey as an example because I would actually swing through the jungle and hide high up on a branch if it meant an hour completely to myself.

Some days I get inspired by the story of Susanna Wesley (mother of Charles and John Wesley, in addition to seventeen other children). She is said to have taught her children to leave her alone if they saw her apron flipped over her head because that meant she was in prayer. This was a woman who knew what was needed for herself and managed it despite terrible hardships and way too many kids. If she could find a way to pray alone in her situation, then surely I can figure out how to meet my personal needs!

Knowing what feeds you, what gives your mind, body, and spirit rest, is the key to finding personal balance. And we are all as unique as the stars in the sky. Each of us is made up of our own needs, and what relaxes me might not be what relaxes you.

I know I need to be alone, but some of my kids are extroverts and they are the opposite. When they start to feel out of balance, they crave time with other people. It's funny when we both are feeling we need to fill that particular tank at the same time. It's like a big joke God is playing on us, me needing to be alone and them needing to be with me. And so you know, their needs win. But that's motherhood and another chapter. Regardless, I will still find ways to satisfy my need to be alone, even if it means having just ten minutes here and there. Sometimes you gotta go for quality over quantity.

I fill my introvert tank because I know that taking care of myself is important. Do you realize that in God's eyes you are as valuable as your children and your husband? I know, it's shocking because we basically walk around our house cleaning up after all of them and gave up our bodies for their very existence. But you are greatly loved by the God of the universe just for being you. Wow!

In his book *He Loves Me!*, Wayne Jacobsen wrote, "If you've never known the joy of simply living in God's acceptance instead of trying to earn it, your most exciting days in Christ are ahead of you. People who learn to live out of a genuine love relationship with the God of the universe will live in more power, more joy, and more righteousness than anyone motivated by fear of his judgment."[1]

When our family was young, we didn't have extra money or anyone to watch our kids, so I had to be creative about getting my "Lisa time." During the kids' naptimes I would have a little quiet time of my own, or in the afternoons I would take the kids outside and I could read while they played. Often my husband would take over for half an hour when he got home from work in the evenings so I could take a shower or sit by myself. Hey, I took what I could get and made the most of it. Playing praise music in the bathroom works in a pinch.

As the kids got older, it became easier to get out of the house for an hour. But I still had to make sure they were taken care of and had their school and chore assignments or I would come home to more unexpected work than was worth the effort. Kids tend to make messes when you're not looking.

If you are an extrovert and need people time, then find a way to get that for yourself several times a week. Try arranging a regular playdate at the park with a friend. Make it easy, no big plans or details that could get in the way. If you have to come up with a picnic or look nice every time you meet, then it defeats the purpose. Just look for simple ways to fill that need for yourself.

Extroverts need people time, I get that. Just because I don't need it to feel refreshed doesn't make it wrong. It's just one of many examples of how what balances me won't always be what balances you.

BODY

A few years ago I had been noticing a downward spiral in my health. I was tired all the time, I couldn't think clearly or remember anything, and I was overweight. I had visited several doctors, who all told me it was just my age, but I knew I needed more than simply to lose the weight. I needed to start feeding my body in a way that sharpened my mind and encouraged my muscles and helped me stay awake after three o'clock in the afternoon.

Left to my own cravings, I would not be a health nut. In fact, I am more of a "doughnuts for breakfast and ice cream for dinner" type of girl. But I know it's not good for me, and I am worth more than artificial flavors and sugar. Soda, cookies, fried foods, chips all can feel satisfying for a short time, but the truth we all know is that they don't really love us as we love them. They're like that bad boyfriend in the seventh grade who says he loves you then dumps you a week later for the cute girl who was mean to you. He isn't even capable of loving you, and neither are potato chips.

What does love you are green veggies and protein. That's a forever kind of love.

So I made some changes. I don't want to go into too much detail because I am not here to promote any specific diet plan. What I do want to tell you is that I removed all the junk from my diet and almost immediately noticed a change in my energy, my mental clarity, and my weight. It is hard to believe how much what we feed our bodies influences every area of our bodies' function.

If you struggle, as I do, to take good care of your body, then it's time for us to stand up together and declare our independence from foods that hate us. In fact, it's important to remember who your body belongs to.

John Dunlop, MD, in his book *Wellness for the Glory of God*, said this:

> We must be careful how we use the phrase "my body," for in truth it belongs to God. He has entrusted its care to us. He expects us to keep it healthy, clean, and fit for his residence and use. There can be no pulling punches here—that is a very strong reason to pursue physical wellness. Paul wrote, "I discipline my body and keep it under control" (1 Cor. 9:27).[2]

And I can't leave the body section of this chapter without talking about exercise. I cannot stress enough how much I have always despised exercising. I don't like to sweat and, while I do enjoy being outdoors, I don't really like moving all that much. The hammock is where it's at for me. It's sad to admit, but in order for you to fully appreciate what I am about to tell you, I do not want to understate the extreme nature of my laziness.

One morning a couple of weeks after I started changing the way I ate, I woke up early. I didn't know why really. I hadn't planned it. But there I was, wide awake at 6:00 a.m. and I had this crazy thought, *I should go for a walk.* Now, I don't know where it came from and I kind of laughed at myself the minute the thought passed, but I couldn't shake it.

I had not considered exercise before. We couldn't afford to go to a gym, and even if we could, the nearest one was miles away and the commute would take too long before my responsibilities of the day started. We didn't have any gym equipment either. In the ten years we had lived in our house, I don't think I had ever stepped foot on the road before that morning.

I got up and started rummaging through my closet to find something to wear. What does one wear for a walk on the road at 6:00 in the morning? I didn't own workout clothes or proper shoes, so I dug up an old pair of maternity leggings and an oversized T-shirt and headed out the door.

After about a quarter mile of walking, I felt so tired that I decided to turn around and head back. What a dumb idea that was! I was never going to try it again. But then the next morning came and I woke up early. I wondered if I could go any farther, so I tried it. And I did the same the next day, and the next, until I was firmly in a routine of walking every morning. Eventually it turned into a light jog, and now I have done a few 5Ks. I may not look the part, but I have actually become an exercise girl.

Now, let me tell you what it did for me. First, the most obvious part is I got more physically fit. I started easily keeping up with my kids. I noticed I wasn't getting winded when we did field trips, such as touring the state capitol (which has lots of stairs) or going to theme parks. I lost weight, but even better than that was I felt so much better than before. And that was not the only result. I also noticed how much I looked forward to having that time with God every morning. I made music playlists for each month and spent time just praising and praying. Since I started this routine I have gone through some very difficult situations, and having that time with Him every morning has been what has helped the most.

"In the spiritual sense, when I'm not taking care of my body, I feel much more weighed down by my stress and problems. I have less energy to serve God and more thorny emotions to wade through when processing life," said Lysa TerKeurst in *Made to Crave*.[3]

Another vital part of self-balance is sleep. If you struggle with sleep, then you are in good company. Most women deal with this at some point in their lives. Sleep has been a struggle for me for most of my adult life. I just don't sleep well naturally, and I made a conscious decision not to use any kind of sleep medication. That just wasn't the road I wanted to take.

I know how much my body needs sleep to function, so I keep a close watch for times when I get low. I use essential oils and breathing exercises to help me sleep. Sometimes when I wake up in the middle of the night with my mind racing, I will grab a pen and paper and write it all down. There are lots of natural tricks to helping you sleep, and I have found that they really do work. You need it!

There are plenty of other areas of bodily care to consider as well. Skin care, supplements, water intake, and relaxation are just a few of the things you may want to integrate into your life when you are attending to the needs of your body. Some people lean toward eating all organic, and others will find proper moisturizing vital for feeling good. We need to give each other room to find our own level of what is important and how to do it. Listen to your instincts and don't give up on yourself. You can do this!

SPIRIT

The last area of "me" that needs attention is my spirit. This isn't where we talk about church and mission trips, but just the very deep, personal area of our connection with God.

Hebrews 4:12 says, "For the word of God is living and active, sharper than any two-edged sword, piercing to the division of soul and of spirit, of joints and of marrow, and discerning the thoughts and intentions of the heart."

The mind and spirit are not the same. My mind is my thoughts, how I learn, and where my emotions are contained. But my spirit is the part of me that connects with the Holy Spirit, leaps with joy when I read the Bible, and will survive beyond my death. It is hard to discern where the mind ends and the spirit begins because we can't see them. I don't try to get too deep about it, but I just make sure I am attending to the needs of them all. And of course what benefits one will help the others also.

My spirit can be filled with love and peace despite what else is happening in my life. Have you ever had to face a conversation you knew was going to be rough, maybe with a friend who had been gossiping about you or with a boss who was about to reprimand you? You didn't want to go into the room, your body was shaky, and your nerves were shot. It can be hard to control your emotions during those times, but if your spirit is at peace, you can get through it with grace and self-control. Before the meeting, instead of completely focusing on being physically rested and mentally prepared, be sure to spend some time in prayer and praise. Just flip open your Bible and see what God has to say. He has wisdom for you there, even if it isn't what you want to hear. Your spirit will find comfort when the rest of you can't.

Feeding your spirit is simple: read the Bible, pray, and praise. Do it whenever works best for you and for however long you can. There is no right or wrong here. My way is just what works for me. Similar to the diet plan, I can't tell you what method will work for you, and frankly, it doesn't matter. Pray in the bathroom first thing in the morning if that is all the time you can eke out. I've been there!

The thing about the spirit is that if you take good care of that part of yourself, it will begin, with maturity, to lead the other parts of you.

When I am in a life crisis, I will fall apart in body and mind, but my spirit doesn't crumble. It is such a deep place of myself that it can't be touched by what others say about me or how much ice cream I eat. My spirit, in connection with the Holy Spirit, can always find peace and joy.

THE HOLY SPIRIT CONNECTION

The only way to really have this kind of peace is through your salvation. If you are truly a Christian and have the assurance of your salvation, then you have that connection with the Holy Spirit. If you don't know if you are saved, then look for evidence in the fruit you are producing. Have you accepted Christ as your Lord and Savior? Do you have a deep, true, dependent, thankful, humble desire for God's ways and not your own? Is there a true joy and trust even though on the surface you are feeling worried or fearful? Does reading God's Word give you a sense of comfort that is beyond understanding?

Your spirit is the part of you that will live beyond your mind and body. Your salvation, the acceptance of Christ as your Savior, is what connects your spirit to God.

If you haven't accepted Him, I pray that you will. There are Christians around you who would love to tell you more about Christ and share with you their testimonies of how He redeemed their own spirits and gave them a love that they never understood before. If you don't know anyone like that, then you can be the first. Start a movement!

All you have to do is ask Him and open your spirit up to His leading.

If you have accepted Christ and you're still not experiencing that depth of joy, this is the time to start nurturing your spirit. It may take some letting go of ideas that have been rooted in you through pain or a difficult upbringing. Those roots are hard to get rid of, but I am here to tell you through my own victories that it is possible. God wants to help you let those pains go and move on with true and meaningful balance in your life.

Balancing is hard; I must say it. I don't want to give you shallow promises. Nothing about getting yourself to balance is easy. Like anything else worth doing, it can be a challenge. But again, *you are worth* the effort!

You are worth being free of hate. You are worth complete joy. You are worth peace in hard times. You, and you alone, are worth my efforts to write this entire book. You are worth Christ's death and resurrection.

Know God, answer His call, invite Him to be the lead of your life. That is the only way to real health and true joy.

TIME TO START

Let's take the seven steps to balance and put them into practice with this first and most important area in our lives. Remember, BALANCE: begin, assess, learn, account, notify, change, endure.

Let's start with the outside, body. I'm gonna use weight as my example because it is a common issue. The pressure to be thin and adorable is intense, and taking that first step to just begin can be stupidly hard. The old joke about starting a diet every Monday is *real!*

BEGIN: Even if you do start a new diet every week, that doesn't make you a failure. As long as you keep trying, keep starting again, keep believing you can, you're doing better than most people.

Don't be defeated by your past failures. They were stepping-stones to reach this point. Decide to start *now*.

ASSESS: Looking at your problem with open eyes and saying "Yes, I *do* eat too much pizza" is hard. But you have to be clear about what it is you want and make sure it is what you should want. If your thought is *I want a perfect body*, then you will never find balance. It isn't possible, and it sets you up to fail. If you can't possibly reach a goal, then you can never have a good perspective on success. You will always fall short and be constantly discouraged. What if you reshaped the goal into something doable, such as "I want to lose fifteen pounds so that I can fit more easily into my clothes"? Begin with knowing what it is you really want, which is likely something deeply personal, and wrap your plans around that instead of reaching for something unattainable, like never eating pizza again.

LEARN: There are so many books and experts out there on weight loss and fitness that it makes my head spin. Many of them have great tips and recipes, and some of them are wackadoos. You have to be discerning and know what is truly best for your body and your lifestyle. Keeping your assessment in mind will help you stay away from those "Lose Fifty Pounds in Two Weeks!" kinds of diets. We are looking for health, not perfection. Carefully teach yourself about good eating plans.

Oftentimes we think the Bible has nothing to say about our problems. I mean, it never says, "A woman should weigh between

125 and 135 pounds." But the truth is that it addresses everything that is important and God didn't accidentally leave any subject out. The Bible is the inerrant Word of God, and if He didn't address a specific topic, that means we didn't need it to be addressed. We have to trust that He told us everything we need to know. It does, in fact, have a lot to say about how God sees us and how He looks at our hearts (1 Sam. 16:7), how we shouldn't be anxious about our bodies (Matt. 6:25), and how focusing on external adorning is vain (Prov. 31:30). That alone tells us that our looks should not be the focus of how we take care of our bodies. Believe me, I like to look pretty just as much as the next girl, but it should not be the focus of my heart. My goal, in our example of trying to lose fifteen pounds, should be for the sake of other things, such as long-term health, wellness, and strength. God also makes it clear that our strength comes from Christ and not ourselves. Don't think you can do this without faith; it won't last.

Account: My husband is an accountant, so he likes to say to me, "The only way to know if something is working is if you keep track of it in some way." (PS: I hate when he tells me that, even though he is right.) Of course, one easy way to measure how your diet is doing is with pounds. But there are other ways also, like how your clothes fit, your energy levels, how easily you move around the house, etc. The scale can be your friend as long as you keep a healthy perspective. No matter what it says in the beginning, you are on a path to taking better care of your body, so you will want to check that measurement regularly. Or try on those tighter clothes every couple of weeks or so to see if they're getting looser. If you don't, you won't know if what you are changing is working.

NOTIFY: Accountability is vital when you're planning to make big changes, especially when they involve taking away some of our comfort. Don't tell yourself that you just want to keep this a secret. Be honest with yourself that you know it's because you might fail and you don't want anyone else to see. It's a leap of faith to tell someone your goals. They can get obnoxious and make you uncomfortable. But it's for your own good! Tell a friend or join a group (you might even make one yourself). When I started my weight-loss journey, I made a Facebook group for women trying to get healthy. They help me so much, and as hard as it is, I tell them when I am not sticking to my plan and they hold me accountable.

CHANGE: Now is the best part, the action. It's time to step out and *do* something about our issue. Buy the foods that are on the plan you chose, join a group, take a walk, get an app to keep up with your progress, and start your journey toward that fifteen-pound loss. It's daily, sometimes minute by minute, but just start. Right now. Not Monday. I am right there with you!

ENDURE: Be sure to prepare for endurance and patience. You aren't going to lose fifteen pounds in two days, and some days you won't lose any weight at all. It may seem to take forever for those old jeans to fit. That's okay. You are still moving toward the place you set for yourself. Be patient with the process. Taking care of your body is a lifelong journey, not a one-week battle. Discouragement is the devil's best weapon against your success in this area, and you now know how to beat him at his own game by believing in what you can do through Christ!

SPIRITUAL DRYNESS

But what if we are working on a different part of ourselves? What if the lack of balance is in my spiritual health? Well, it's the same process.

BEGIN: Realize that you need to stay healthy in this area. Women get so busy that we think we can ignore our spiritual health, and that can be dangerous. If you've let this slip, it's time this second to start turning that around.

ASSESS: Take a step back and see if you can figure out the problem. Do you feel dry spiritually, not experiencing the satisfaction of the living water? See it for what it is, a season of dryness. Let yourself try to identify some of the problem. Have you had a crisis? Are you depressed? Do you feel grief over something, even something small? What do you think is missing?

LEARN: What does God have to say about spiritual dryness? We know that He is always there to satisfy our thirst (John 7:37) and that the Holy Spirit is there to remind us of God (John 14:26). There is *a lot* to say about our relationship with God, and just reading it is *so* encouraging! Often just being in His Word is enough to quench that thirst. He is always there and ready to give us grace, peace, and mercy.

ACCOUNT: How do we measure spiritual dryness? Well, when was the last time you felt fulfilled in your relationship with God? Can you remember a time of joy and peace? What do you think helped you feel close to Him then? Think on how that felt, and see if there is a way to work your way back to that. Are you feeling tired or overwhelmed with your life and not finding time to spend with Him? Time is a measurement we can use here. If nothing else, dedicate a certain amount of time to working on your relationship with God each day. You could measure this need by how quickly you recover from a struggle. Does it take you longer than you would like to bounce back after an unexpected crisis? Choose some ways to measure your problem, and see if you can set small goals to improve that.

I love, *love* how Emily P. Freeman put it in her book *Grace for the Good Girl*: "For me, life was pretty well put together. I did life right. I went to church regularly. I got married and had babies in the appropriate order. I never got arrested. I recycled. I loved Jesus. But sometimes in the quiet stillness, I felt an aching that wouldn't go away, a longing to *taste and see*, to live authentically free. My instinctive impulse was to find my worth in the response of people around me, and as a result, people became measuring sticks for my goodness rather than unique expressions of God."[4]

Notify: Do not, I repeat, *do not* try to do this on your own! The devil loves to keep us isolated and convince us that we are the only person with this problem. My beloved, you are not alone in your struggle. You probably have a dozen friends who are dealing with a very similar issue, or have at one time, and would completely understand. Find a few trusted people to share your problem with and tell them what you think you need to do. Let them speak wisdom into your life, and take that wisdom and ask God to illuminate what you have to learn from them. Check in with them; don't be shy if they don't call you first and ask how you are. Not everyone is gifted at that, so don't let that stop you from continuing to hold yourself up to them for accountability.

Change: Now, after all of that preparation, do you have any ideas of how you might make some changes to rebalance this area of your life?

Endure: Now be patient. The change won't happen overnight (although this is the one area that can actually transform instantly; God is amazing like that!). If it is slow, it is because you need to keep working through the steps and focusing on this. Your spiritual life is nothing to take lightly; it can make the difference in every other area of your life!

ASSIGNMENT

Each morning for a week when you get up, think of one part of *you* where you'd like to find a better balance. You don't have to tell anyone yet; just think on it or journal about it. This is a time of thinking and letting God show you where your focus is best used. Now, dedicate five minutes to praying for God to give you wisdom for this week. I mean it. Set your timer and go hide in the closet for five minutes. Ask Him to point out where you need to see things differently, to show you verses that will inspire you to change, and to bring people across your path who will set great examples. He can do anything if you are open! The next week, try it again with a different small decision. Don't focus on the same area two weeks in a row. We need to relax and let things soak in to really find true, lifelong balance.

BEING MARRIED

*He who finds a wife finds a good thing and
obtains favor from the LORD.*

Proverbs 18:22

DATE NIGHT

James and I have always believed in the power of a weekly date
night. He usually "asks me out" and we make simple plans. When
the kids were little, we couldn't afford to eat in a restaurant *and*
hire a babysitter, so I would settle the kids into bed early and he
would go pick up takeout from our favorite Mexican restaurant
(a life without Mexican food is no life at all, amen?). We would
usually eat dinner in our comfy chairs in the bedroom and just
talk. We might rent a movie or listen to music or play a card game,
but typically we just talked.

One Friday night we had decided it was a good night to stay
in for our date. We got a pizza and ate in our bedroom. We often
like to sit in there to talk and just be together while lounging in our
overstuffed, ridiculously comfortable matching recliners. On this
night we chatted about the week and shared a laugh or two. We
were both in a pretty good mood, and I guess he must have been
feeling frisky because after we finished eating he said to me, "Hey,
why don't you come here and sit with me in my chair?"

Um, he had never asked me that before. I am not really the sit-on-your-lap kind of girl. I am more of a you-can-flirt-with-me-from-over-there person. Plus, neither of us is what you would consider small. We both needed to lose a few pounds, or twenty, and I wasn't sure if the chair could handle it. My thoughts immediately flashed to broken chairs, a trip to the emergency room, and shattered bones ending with James in a wheelchair for the rest of his life. Of course, that whole picture took 1.3 seconds to come together in my mind.

"No thanks," I said, "it wouldn't be very comfortable."

"Aw, come on. It'll be nice. I want to sit with you."

"Nah," I replied. "I will hurt you."

"No, you won't!" he said. "Come on over here."

I kept rejecting him and he kept insisting until I finally gave in. I said something supersweet like, "Oh. Alright. Fine."

I hesitantly stood up from my chair and made my way over to him. I winced as I crawled into his lap. I said things like, "It's going to mess up my bad knee," "This will bother my neck," and, "I'm going to hurt you."

I can't help but stop here and say how lucky he is to be married to such a cheerful, loving, romantic woman.

We sat there for, oh, about a minute and a half and just as I was starting to think this might not have been the terrible idea I originally assumed, he got a cramp in his foot. Concerned that this might put to death any hope of me ever sitting in his lap again, he tried to keep me from knowing about it. He kept shifting around until finally he blurted out, "I need to move; I have a *cramp*!"

And without actually getting up, I started to laugh. This was no gentle, ladylike laughter. This was full-on guffawing. At first it annoyed him because he was starting to feel the pain from the foot cramp, but he couldn't help but get caught up in the humor of the situation, which was about to get much worse.

We were both cracking up and trying to get ourselves out of the chair, only to discover that the laughing and wiggling had apparently shifted us lower in the seat and we were wedged in. We could *not* get up. Which caused us to laugh harder and harder until, well, you know what happens when a forty-five-year-old woman who has had nine babies laughs uncontrollably.

I couldn't hold it in! He felt the warm moisture on his leg and shouted with a slight panic in his voice, "What did you do? Did you just pee on me?" I couldn't even stop laughing enough to answer, but it was obvious. He couldn't decide if he should be horrified or amused. I have to admit; it was a toss-up for me too.

Eventually we got out of the chair, changed clothes, and went back to sitting in our individual recliners. But we will never forget that night. I think we would both say it was honestly one of the best, most romantic evenings we have ever had.

It doesn't get much better than that.

MARRIAGE IS FULL OF SURPRISES

Marriage is a lot like our time together in the recliner. We try to keep the fire going, but sometimes we just get stuck.

My husband, James, and I recently celebrated our thirtieth wedding anniversary. We have had plenty of falls and hard times, but I would say it's been mostly laughing and enjoying the bumps along the road.

As wonderful as it is, marriage is the hardest relationship you will ever have. It is also the most valuable. It changes us, challenges us, stretches us, and refines us. Marriage is the single most character-building aspect of your life, and it is a gift from God to make you holier. Hard? Uh, yeah. But so, so, so worth the effort.

I love the book *Sacred Marriage* by Gary Thomas. He said this about the value of the marriage relationship:

> I *love* marriage, and I love *my* marriage. I love the fun parts, the easy parts, and the pleasurable parts, but also the difficult parts—the parts that help me understand myself and my spouse on a deeper level; the parts that are painful but crucify the parts of me that I hate; the parts that force me to my knees and teach me that I need to learn to love with God's love instead of just trying harder. Marriage has led me to deeper levels of understanding, more pronounced worship, and a sense of fellowship that I never knew existed.[1]

Personally, I don't like to change and grow. I resist changing my mind about something the same way my husband resists buying new clothes. I am doing perfectly fine the way I am right now, *thank you very much.* But it turns out that sometimes I am wrong. I know, shocking. And sometimes even if I am not wrong, I can go ahead and let my husband have his way just because, well, I love him. It is not easy for my stubborn self to admit, but down deep I have a lot of room to grow still.

WHAT IS A BALANCED MARRIAGE ANYWAY?

Really, we don't want our marriage to be easy and effortless. The work and the trials are where the passion and fulfillment come from. I'm only an expert in my own marriage, but after twenty-nine years we still have our ups and downs. It's just the maturity and knowing each other well have made the rises more enjoyable and the falls less upsetting. I know that even if we argue or have a problem, it will pass. And I know that the good times are as much a part of the journey together and I trust them to come back even when they disappear.

If you're feeling lonely or hurt or confused or angry on a regular basis within your marriage, you need to get some balance.

Being balanced means that when the hard times come you know what to grab on to so you don't fall. You have a net that will stop you if you go too close to the edge. The net is your faith and your ability to find safety. It is not letting any time pass when you realize there is a problem. You follow the BALANCE steps and get yourself back to a place where you can jump without risking life and limb.

Isn't it funny how we feel completely off in every area when our marriage is not healthy? If I think my husband is annoyed by me, I can't seem to focus on other things. I know he is the same way. But we do get upset, so we have to make sure we pull back in and do what is necessary to change it.

I talk to many women who have really difficult marriages. They feel as though they are close to walking away and ending the relationship. I want to say to those of you who are there: don't hide from the world and think you can handle this on your own. Talk to someone, and not your family. I urge you to work hard at not talking trash about your husband while you go through the difficult process of deciding what to do with your marriage. Even if you feel like it's the end, please go through the BALANCE steps and see what you can learn from your situation.

TRY TRUST

It starts with trust. Look, I am the worst at trusting someone, even my husband. I am far too self-protective. Even all these years later I am carrying around some of the baggage that I brought into our relationship. But I know that it's an area that I must be constantly working on to keep my marriage strong. My husband works hard at being a person who deserves to be trusted. That, in turn, makes me want to trust him for his efforts even though he can't be perfect at it. Get on the cycle of trust now, and let it start to do its work. Be willing to give more trust in small ways, and work at being more trustworthy.

Once that begins to blossom, work on having faith in your spouse. You married this person, and now it is time to believe they can be everything you saw in them from the beginning. It's hard to look at the overweight guy in the recliner with his belt unbuckled and a stain on his shirt and see that young man who was going to take on the world. He is in there. Maybe he got lost along the way, and maybe he is exhausted from the unexpected responsibilities that got thrown his way over the years, but that cute guy you married is there. Have faith in him, let him know you believe he can do great things, and release the bitterness you feel because he didn't keep every promise. Remember, faith is believing in what you can't see. Have faith in what your spouse can do, and look for ways to instill confidence instead of disappointment.

No matter what your issue is, you can find ways to straighten out some of the bad habits and wrong turns. Let's work on some ways that you can pull yourself into more than "how it used to be." Let's find ways to make it better!

FINDING YOUR BALANCE

BEGIN: You have to start. Giving up is so tempting when you feel hurt or disappointed. I beg of you, don't! Believe in what your marriage can be and that you can make personal changes that will turn the tide.

ASSESS: What is the real problem here? What do you think is your contribution to the problem? It's easy to think of how the other person needs to change, but let's just focus on you. Be honest with yourself and ask God to show you some blind spots that you aren't seeing. We all have blind spots, especially in our marriages. A trusted friend, counselor, or pastor can help you see these. This is not necessarily the same as the accountability relationship, but more of an adviser who may speak only occasionally into your life.

If you're anything like me, you might get a *liiittle* bit defensive when it is suggested that you are part of the problem. Say what? Perfect me? So when I get advice, I like to give it twenty-four hours for the idea to settle in before I make any plans or decisions. Most of the time that is enough for me to see my own flawed reasoning.

LEARN: There's no question that God has much to say about our marriage relationships. Some of it is not what I want to hear, but I have to believe that if He said it, then it is for my good. One thing to remember when looking into God's Word is that it is inerrant (without error). Believing that is at the core of really finding the kind of balance we are talking about here. So when it says words like *submit* and *love*, it means it fully.

Submission is a touchy subject and I am not going to dig deep into it, but I do want to encourage you as a wife that it is a blessing to submit. Being submissive is not a sign that you are weak; in fact, it is a strength that most women will never experience. You have opinions and are often right, and you should be honest with your husband for sure! But in the end if he makes a decision that you disagree with, you are wise to submit and pray and trust God. We need to know that submitting to our husband is not about him being right, but about him being the leader that God placed in our home. My husband, James, braces himself when I say to him, "Hey! Can we talk for a minute? I have an idea!" I could be about to tell him anything from "Let's sell the house and live in an RV!" to "I want to teach the boys karate." Really, my ideas are totally unpredictable. He politely listens, then carefully throws his cold water of logic and practicality on my excitement.

He never seems to be as excited about my ideas as I am. Imagine that!

I have learned not to let his lack of enthusiasm upset or irritate me. May you learn now what took me at least twenty years to figure out. I will thank him for listening, then ask God to either help me let go of my idea or help James start to like it. Either way, I can trust God with my husband and submit to him.

Sometimes issues are bigger than a wild hair of an idea. You might even be right about what is best for your family, which is why it is even more important to know what the Bible says and keep being open to learning. I want to encourage you to pay attention to how argumentative you are when your husband makes a decision you don't like. Watch your heart attitude, and be careful not to put him down or give the impression that you think your way is the only way. If this is a struggle for you (as it is for most of us!), then ask God to help you slowly find ways to submit and trust.

ACCOUNT: Good grief! How will we measure marriage unhappiness? Well, there actually is a way! Think length and breadth.

How deep and wide is the problem? Does it fill the room, last for hours, linger for days? That will help you figure out the size of the necessary solution.

For example, if you argue every night when he walks in the door because you each think the other should take care of dinner, then you can see that it is a daily issue. Time is a measuring tool. Second, do you stew over it all afternoon before he gets home, feeling irritated and dreading the argument you know is coming? That's a wider issue. Then, does it last all night, both of you fuming at being misunderstood and thinking the other doesn't care? That is a wide breadth. It takes up half of your day. So your solution should be similarly sized. You will want to have your plan to pull your marriage back to a place of evening peace to cover all of these areas. Instead of measuring only the argument, measure its entire effect from early afternoon until bedtime.

You could look at how long you argue, how loud it gets, where you argue, how long you stay mad, how many times you say something too harsh; you could even target the idea of finding places in the argument when you could stop and apologize and then keep going. Find something you can actually count, and then see if you can find ways to reduce that number.

What if, instead of watching only your own happiness in the relationship, you looked for ways to measure your spouse's? When you are together, count how many times he seems frustrated or irritated. Or if you notice him being negative in his comments about what you are talking about, keep track of how often he does that. Don't tell him; just make a mental note. Then decide you want to lower that number. Or another idea is to think of it like thunder and lightning. In a storm, the longer the space of time between the thunder and the lightning, the farther away the storm is. So this could be the same: the longer you go without feeling lonely or hurt, the farther away the problem is.

I really like the book *Boundaries in Marriage* by Dr. Henry Cloud and Dr. John Townsend. It has some wonderful tips and tricks to making marriage work. This favorite quote applies well to my point here of measuring and paying attention:

> If you don't have power to change your spouse, what *do* you have power over? You have the power to confess, submit, and repent of your own hurtful ways in your marriage. You can identify these hurtful ways, ask God for his help to overcome them, and be willing to change. Whatever your spouse does that bothers you, it's certain that you do things that bother him also. If you want your spouse to listen to your boundaries, ask him where you may be violating his. When you are hurt or upset, you may try to control everything, or you may withdraw into silence. Nothing is more conducive to a spouse's growth than a mate who sincerely wants to change.[2]

Let's agree together that we will work on our attitudes and look for areas to change ourselves, our responses, our defensiveness. You aren't a victim of your relationship; you are half of it.

I want to be clear here: no one should stay in an abusive relationship. You, nor your spouse, deserves to be mistreated. Just be careful what you are calling abuse before you act on that notion. Talk to someone and be honest without trying to paint your spouse in a negative light. I am not advocating staying in an abusive situation, but a hard marriage is different than an abusive one.

NOTIFY: Talk to someone about your goals, but I have to issue a caution here. You should never betray your husband's confidence. If you know he would not want you to share something about him with anyone, then don't. When I get out of balance in my marriage, I have one friend whom I will confide in and share with her my new goals for repairing the relationship. My husband knows she is trustworthy, but I still ask him if he minds if I talk to her about whatever we are going through. Be careful not to cut your husband down or be critical of him. You can relate your difficulty in dealing with a situation without revealing his weaknesses. Let's say, for instance, your washing machine needs repairing. If you are arguing because he wants to pull it out and try to fix it himself to save money and you want to buy a new one because this is the sixth time in three months that it has broken down, you can share your struggle with your friend without making him sound like an idiot.

Too many times as women we are ready to jump on our husband's inadequacies with our friends. We like that old *"Men!"*

saying, and it's fun to join together in our mutual issues in dealing with these alien creatures. But, my friend, think of how you would feel if you discovered him talking about you like that. It would hurt! You want to be honoring toward your husband even if he is making choices that you don't understand, even if he is being silly and selfish! Try making it clear that your goal is to build up your marriage *and* be able to do laundry. So when you talk to a friend, make sure you show that you are hoping to lift up your husband but are struggling in this situation.

And one more thought for the road: if your friend tears down your husband, then you need to stop turning to her for this kind of accountability. You need to be sharing with someone who will build you up while you are working on this delicate relationship. Oh, and don't talk to your mom about your husband. Just don't. It's never a good idea.

CHANGE: Now that you have looked at your problem, seen what the Bible says, found a way to measure your goals, and gotten advice, it's time to move ahead. Staying on the subject of building trust and faith in your spouse, this can feel like a scary change. What if I get hurt? What happens when he lets me down? Lord, please don't make me give up any of my control!

Watch how you recoil inside when you are called on to trust your husband. Or when you feel that nudge to believe in a decision he makes and your flesh wants to fight against it. So often we have gotten into habits of responding poorly and it's hard to see when we do it and hard to change it when we finally see it.

Take it one step at a time and keep on truckin'. I believe you can do this!

The next time you feel fear over letting your husband lead, give that fear to God. Just try it; let this man whom you chose to spend your life with hold the reins, and you just relax. Watch him brace for your usual response, and then surprise him.

You saw *Fireproof*, right? Remember how the dad challenged his son to make small changes in his action and attitude toward his wife for forty days? That is the kind of thing I am talking about. But this is more personal to you. You will have to make your own list of things to act on, but I am telling you, this works! I have seen it time and time again in my own marriage and many of my friends'.

ENDURE: This is not a sprint, my friends. This is for life, so the issues don't need to be solved in a day. New issues will pop up and the relationship will grow into something you never imagined on your wedding day. When you feel frustrated with the results of your efforts to make a change in your marriage, be patient. This is two people trying to become one, and it takes a lifetime. Remember, the goal is not perfection, but godliness.

God gets the glory when two very different people are able to build a life together. It is not easy to do that. The challenges you face in your marriage can, with the right attitude and a lot of prayer, make you a stronger, holier version of yourself. Keep your eye on the goal you set when you made your changes, and don't let yourself get sidetracked when your feelings are hurt or it gets hard.

The idea that I am not shooting for happiness but to become more like Christ through my marriage is one that took me time to grasp. It is a beautiful thing, seeing your marriage struggles as opportunities for growth, but it is *so* challenging!

My very favorite quote from *Sacred Marriage* speaks to this concept of the purpose of marriage:

> How can we, as married saints, use the daily rush of activities and the seeming chaos of family life as a reminder of God's presence? To be sure, we have many challenges to overcome, but isn't there a way we can use marriage to draw us closer to God rather than let it dull our senses and lead us into a practical atheism where we give lip service to God but live as if he simply does not exist? Rather than allowing marriage to blunt our sensitivities, can we use it to awaken our souls in new and profound ways?[3]

You can certainly enjoy your marriage, even a hard one. But if you don't look at the deeper purpose, then you are missing one of the great fulfillments in life! Instead of dulling our senses by blaming our problems on others, let's reach for the stars and see God's glory in every trial.

MEETING IN THE MIDDLE

We don't have to agree to have a healthy marriage. In fact, not agreeing is what gives us flavor. If we always had the same ideas, then life would be dull!

I like to do DIY projects, and my husband, well, he's not into them. He doesn't think our house even needs changing, and I think it constantly needs changing. I doubt we will ever meet in the middle. I will probably be trying to tear out walls in our nursing home.

He is always nice just to leave me to my power tools and crazy ideas. I'll go marching across the backyard on my way to my little workshop with a determined look on my face, and he knows to stay *out of the way*. Then, once I finish my project, I beg him to come look at my masterpiece. But he can't just look at whatever my current project is and say, "Great job, hon! I love it." No, he has to inspect every inch while I stand there bracing myself for the constructive comments. One weekend I built a jewelry cabinet for my bathroom that I had been wanting to make for over a year. I sawed and sanded and painted and set it all up, and when I showed him, he took a long look at it and said, "It's not level."

"What? It's *fine*! I love it!"

He asked if I had used a level to install it and I had to admit that I hadn't. I didn't really care; it looked great to me and it was my cabinet for me to use and I didn't want to change it. But he went to get our level and brought it back to hold it up to my work, and there it was: one bubble off.

We stood there, not about to agree on how to handle the situation. He was right that it wasn't level. I was right that it didn't matter for this project. Did we have to agree? No. I just smiled and said I was leaving it that way, and he smiled and said, "Okay."

And that cabinet is still in my bathroom two years later, holding all of my necklaces and not falling apart. So there you go.

REFOCUS YOUR PERSPECTIVE

My goal here is not to solve your marriage problems. My goal is to turn your focus from trying to find that perfect marriage to looking at how seeking balance can beautifully stretch you and help you build strength. I challenge you to see your married life as a blessing to your character development and a lifelong opportunity to grow and learn more about how to have a healthy relationship. We all like the feeling of serving others, but when it comes to our spouse, we tend to slip into the idea that we should be served (and even slightly worshipped) by them. Let's turn our hearts and minds to finding balance not only in our reactions and actions toward our husband, but to our own inner attitudes.

You are not only building a beautiful life for you as a couple but also affecting everyone who is watching you! This is especially true for your children. I once heard someone say, "Be the kind of wife that when your son sees you he thinks, *I've got to get me one of those!*" Ouchie! I don't know if I have been that all the time. I have some pretty selfish moments. It helps me to realize that I am being watched. I don't want my sons to think it's okay to be disrespected because of all the times I showed disrespect to their dad.

My sweet friend Melanie Shankle put it like this in her book *The Antelope in the Living Room*: "Marriage can be the biggest blessing and the most significant challenge two people ever take on. It's the joy of knowing there is someone to share in your sorrows and triumphs and the challenge of living with someone who thinks it's a good idea to hang a giant antelope on your living room wall."[4]

If your marriage has more trial than joy, use that as a measuring tool and ask God to help you find ways to change that statistic. Your marriage is a living entity that needs feeding, nurturing, rest, and breathing room. Don't think that because it has been starved it is beyond salvaging. Start feeding it healthy choices, and watch it come back to health. Nothing is impossible with God!

ASSIGNMENT

I'd like you to try something. On your phone make a note called "Balance." For the next month every time you feel a frustration in your marriage, think of a word that describes your feeling and do a Google search for it like this: "Bible verse about _____." Add in whatever frustration word you felt. "Bible verse about anger," or "Bible verse about loneliness," and so forth. It takes just a second, then copy and paste one of the verses you find into your Balance note.

For example, when I search for "Bible verse about frustration," the first one that comes up is Isaiah 41:10: "Fear not, for I am with you; be not dismayed, for I am your God." Isn't that uplifting! We don't have to fear the unknown or our feelings or what will happen in our marriage. He is with us!

Eventually, you will have built a great list of verses that you can look at and maybe even memorize. Look at that list and find a quick encouragement when you need a way to find balance in your marriage. The notes will remind you of how God gave you peace in the past, and your confidence will grow!

MOTHERHOOD

*Her children rise up and call her blessed; her
husband also, and he praises her.*

Proverbs 31:28

THE BALLET CLASS

When our oldest daughter was five, she desperately wanted to take ballet. So I found a class that one of her friends attended with Christian music and similar values to ours. The problem was that it was forty-five minutes away. But it was Houston, and frankly, that is a short drive when you're in Houston, where it can take half an hour just to get across a street.

Besides a dancing five-year-old, I also had a three-year-old and an eighteen-month-old and I was ready to give birth to child number four any minute. Oh, and did I mention that the class started at 8:30 in the morning? I think I have tried to block it out.

I am a morning person, but that goes out the window when you're extra pregnant with young children. Sleep is rare and your body begs for it like a dog begs for a treat. When the alarm clock blasted me awake in the morning, I'd cry out, "Please, Lord, I will do *anything* for an extra five minutes!"

Between the four of us, we had trouble getting to class on time and it was costing us precious money we really couldn't afford. So I told my daughter that if she wanted to keep going she would have to at least get herself ready to go on time. We had a long talk about it the night before, and I was hopeful for the next day.

But it did not go well. My belly ached and I was grumpy. The eighteen-month-old kept taking her clothes off (she was going through a naked phase), and the three-year-old was poking along like he didn't care at all if we were on time to his sister's ballet class.

I got up early but couldn't seem to get things moving along at the necessary speed, and by the time we got into the minivan ten minutes late, I was done. I was mad at the kids, especially the little ballerina who lost her shoes (that we had laid out the night before) and cried over her breakfast and wouldn't help me redress her sister. This just seemed like something we should be able to do, but hard as I tried, it never happened the way I wanted.

After buckling them all in and wedging myself behind the steering wheel, I just sat there, fuming. I didn't move, boiling with frustration. In what would be remembered for years as "the time Mommy got really mad," I blew. I turned around and started fussing like a hen over her eggs (we live on a hobby farm, so believe me, this is a *lot* of fussing). I told the kids we would quit ballet if this ever happened again, and I just kept going. Fuss, yell, vent, rant.

Their little faces, especially ballerina's, were frozen in shock. They had never been yelled at before and this was epic. The expression on ballerina's face was so exaggerated that it slowed me down until I finally stopped and asked her, "Well? Do you have anything to say?"

She took a breath and slowly raised her right pointer finger to her nose and said quietly, "Mommy, you have a great big booger hanging out of your nose."

There are very few things that could have diffused my irritation at that moment, but that comment did the trick. I mean, who cares about getting to class on time when there's a green-nostril situation? I didn't know whether to be embarrassed or entertained. I went with both.

My behavior that morning was not okay. I blew my nose, then asked for their forgiveness. I never wanted my kids to be traumatized or afraid of me. The humor of the booger helped me see that I was blowing (pun intended) all of this out of proportion.

I turned on some Barney songs and off we headed, late as usual, to ballet. But I had a fresh outlook on the whole thing.

Relax, do your best, be kind, and for heaven's sake … carry Kleenex at all times.

Truly, motherhood should be joy filled, fun, exciting, fulfilling, thrilling, delightful, and good. If you aren't experiencing that, then this is the chapter for you. I promise there is hope, not from me, but from the One who knows all of your sorrow and disappointment and burden.

THE SECRET

This is less of a secret and more of a little-known fact, but here it is. Your peace and joy come from inside of you and not outside. You are not stuck in misery because of your current situation, you don't have to be unhappy just because someone around you is unhappy, and you can have a deep, defining joy even in the hardest of circumstances.

Finding balance in motherhood is not about how well behaved your children are or how happy they are or how well liked. Balance in this area is an inner gift, one that can't be lost no matter what happens around you. Your children need a mom who won't lose her joy even if they act like little monsters every once in a while. Or a lot of the time.

So let's look at motherhood under the microscope of balance. You can't control your kids, even if it is tempting to try sometimes. This is not what you want because they need to make choices for themselves and learn from those choices. You also can't make them happy, as you probably discovered before the end of the first day they were born. How many times did I march around my living room at 3:00 a.m. bouncing my screaming baby and wondering what was wrong with him or her? If my happiness depended on their happiness, I would be in serious trouble.

In her book *Am I Messing Up My Kids? And Other Questions Every Mom Asks*, Lysa TerKeurst said, "When hard times come and beat against our stability, we must be determined to hear God's words and put them into practice. Then nothing can topple our peace, security, or true identity."[1]

I'm not sure who else needed to hear that, but I know I certainly did. So dry your tears, sweet mama. Today is a new day. A day when we will be defined only by God's truth and grace as we navigate this wild wonder called parenthood.

Balance is found in your own joy. This is true in every area of life, but it is especially difficult to find when it comes to our kids. If they are struggling, we feel their agony and it is really hard to let that go. Really hard. Of course you still care about them and empathize with their suffering. It's not lack of love or compassion when you are able to find joy even though someone you love is suffering. It is an understanding of the difference between God's place in your life and theirs. When you find that place of being joy filled despite what your children are experiencing, you will be passing on a gift to them. You are showing your children that they can also have deep joy that can't be shaken by outside circumstances. Hallelujah!

TRY THIS

The next time your child has a meltdown, tell yourself to stay calm and not respond with your own near nervous breakdown. With young children, typically their crying has very little to do with anything real, so you should be able to realize that even if they can't. He wants out of his car seat or she doesn't want to eat the food you served her or the baby is crying for no obvious reason. This is the perfect time to practice being joyful.

Tell yourself, "Nothing is happening except this child is upset. I don't need to get upset too," and just go on with whatever you're doing. You control your own energy in the situation. Take deep breaths, remind yourself of what is true, that everything is fine and you getting upset is only going to make it worse for no reason.

Those 3:00 a.m. crying-baby sessions are the perfect opportunities to teach yourself to relax while your child is feeling stressed. You've checked all the options. Clean diaper, full tummy, no fever; maybe there is something wrong that you can't see, or maybe he's just crying. Do you know that babies actually need to cry for exercise a few times a day? We don't want them to never cry! So just comfort him the best you can and think about other things, praise, smile, pray over him, whatever relaxes you and keeps your heart rate down.

I knew a woman who would go into a tizzy every time her baby cried. Her voice would instantly get high pitched, she would speed up her movements, and it looked like she was in a panic (the mom, not the baby). I asked her one day, "What are you so distraught about?"

She told me her baby crying got her all upset, and when she couldn't stop it, she would become more and more agitated. I asked her if she had ever tried making herself calm down when the crying started and maybe that would actually help the baby. She looked at me like I had three heads. But a few weeks later she pulled me aside at church and thanked me for the suggestion. She thought it was crazy at first but decided to try it. She made herself stay calm when her baby cried, and she said, "You know what happened? He only cried for about two minutes, then stopped! Usually he cries for an hour!"

She kept on teaching herself to stay calm and I could not believe the change in her baby; it was kind of remarkable!

Of course, the testimony of one person is not a scientific study. But I promise you that if you are getting wound up when your children cry or fuss, then you are making the problem worse. God is clear with us about the subjects of anxiety and fretting. Psalm 37:8 reads, "Refrain from anger, and forsake wrath! Fret not yourself; it tends only to evil."

OLD HABITS DIE HARD

Once the kids are older and we have built a relationship with them, it can be even harder to change our responses. We get into habits and find ourselves instantly becoming frustrated or irritated with the things they do. If you get annoyed with your children, it is normal! You aren't the only mom who ever felt worn out from all the childish behavior coming from these little people.

I want to pause and address the topic of anger. Acting out in anger, my dear friend, is a sin. If you are lashing out in anger toward your children, then let's talk about ways you can stop that. I have done it; all moms have. I am not talking to you from a place of innocence. You are forgiven. Right here. Right now. Totally forgiven.

It becomes a habit. The child may be the instigator, but we participate in it and are fully responsible for our behavior. We feel the tension before the explosion. Many of us have some strong-willed kids, and they tend to make it even harder to keep the peace. But believe me, that child who is defensive, angry, and mean is nothing more than a hurting soul, and it's our job to do what we can to heal that hurt. Lashing back is not going to help. Firmness with gentleness and humility is the answer.

One thing that will help to break the habit of reacting in anger is stopping yourself before it gets bad. Right when you sense that familiar feeling of anger welling up, stop immediately. Don't wait until it has taken over you and you get that feeling like you can't control it. It's similar to any sin—it's easier to stop in the beginning than later when it has become a monster.

When I get really frustrated with my kids, I make myself step away from the situation for a minute. It helps so much! I can take a breath, look at the situation for what it really is—usually a kid with an attitude problem—make a reasonable plan (which sometimes means talking to another adult for insight), and enter back calmer. I will sometimes tell my child, "I am angry with you, and I don't want to hurt your feelings because I love you. So let's talk about this more later and for now you may do _____." I try to think of a task or simple assignment that will give them something to do while I process the problem and ask God for insight.

It takes time, chipping away at habits you've created with your child. It is worth every effort at turning your reactions around even though it's hard. You will be helping your child see that even old people can change.

EVERY DAY IS A BALANCING ACT

With motherhood, the challenge of balancing is daily, hourly, minutely. The subjects in the other chapters in this book can have times when they are so easy to balance and can even go a year without too many trials. But not motherhood. Nope. It's constant.

Kids, unfortunately, are not born very mature. I mean, they poop at inopportune times and they won't eat what you feed them and they kick you when you try to get them in the minivan, a car you really didn't want in the first place. Plus, they don't even seem the least bit grateful for the money you spent on them that you could have spent on a much sportier vehicle.

But we keep having more kids and keep putting ourselves through the agony. Why? Because we dreamed of this all our lives, of course. And the moms on TV made it look so easy.

In real life, motherhood problems don't get solved in half an hour and no one ever prepares you for the feeling of standing in front of a firing squad at snacktime if you ran out of Goldfish.

The war is not with the kids; it is with our own nature. In any other relationship, if I make someone a peanut butter and jelly sandwich, they will thank me and eat it. But the parent-child relationship is a whole other animal. If I make my own child a sandwich, she feels perfectly free to push it away and demand something else. I want to say, "Excuse me? I am sick and busy and killed myself over that sandwich!" But I don't because I am the mom. I am supposed to tolerate and teach.

If you think I am being too hard, try this on for size from John Rosemond's *Parenting by the Book: Biblical Wisdom for Raising Your Child*: "Likewise, the micromanaging, short-term-oriented parent frequently complains about how her children stress her out, how they are 'difficult,' how they never give her a moment's peace, and the like. She doesn't realize that the problem is not her children—it's her."[2]

Bam! Tell it like it is, John. We need to hear the truth before we lose our sanity. Or our family.

And you really never know when it is going to happen. Oh sure, some things are expected. If your child protests every time you tell him to take a bath, then you can kind of brace yourself. But when you are ten minutes late for the dentist and he spills a whole box of crackers on the floor (why was he eating crackers anyway?) and the dog rushes in and starts eating the crumbs, suddenly without any warning, you are in a crisis situation.

How do you find balance with *that*?

YEP, IT'S STILL YOU

It goes right back to the understanding that *you* are the determining factor in how a situation will go. How you think about life, what God has given you, who you are as a person, who your children are in God's eyes, and what your purpose is will determine how quickly you can recover from a spill.

Do you know that there are only 940 Saturdays from the time your child is born until he or she is eighteen? And 260 of them are gone by your child's fifth birthday. Waaahhh! I could cry just thinking about it. It is such a short amount of time. Let's not waste it by blowing up over little things and letting spilled crackers ruin our days.

How do you think of life? Is it a gift? Do you thank God for it every single morning? Being aware of the value of life, both yours and your child's, is essential to changing your attitude about hard situations. You can see even the spills as gifts. You get to stop whatever you're doing and teach a lesson on whatever needs to be done to clean up the mess. You can spot a weak area in your child and make plans to work on that (as in, eats crackers when he's supposed to be putting his shoes on). Every obstacle is an opportunity for something!

What has God given you? Oh my word, *so much*! If you are reading this book, then you have been given more than most people in the whole world! Not because of this book, but because you own any books at all, because you can read, because you get to learn how to grow in your faith through freedom, because you have half an hour to spend on yourself, and the list goes on. See what God has given you? Ask Him to open your eyes. Everything around you is a gift, even the hard things.

In *How to Ruin Your Child in Seven Easy Steps*, Patrick M. Quinn and Ken Roach wrote:

> That's what patience is all about: Believing that the struggle—and pain—are not only necessary evils in a fallen world but are actually doorways through which we enter into our greatest joys. For the Christian, that belief is based on our trust that God loves us enough not to allow anything to come our way that He cannot use for our greater good.[3]

Who are you? You are a child of the King, you were created for a purpose, you are blessed among women, you are beautiful and talented and amazing. You have the capability to be a light for this world through your faith, and you are a gift to your children.

Who are your children? Gifts, not just to you, but to the world. Your children can be world changers, life explorers, and hopefully

Christ followers. They are special, brilliant, beautiful, and talented, and you are not the only one who sees that. God sees, other people see, and He is preparing a path for each of them filled with people who will serve their lives in some way. Don't ever forget that you being their mom is only a part of their identities.

What is your purpose? In three words, to glorify God.

FINDING BALANCE

BEGIN: Let's just say it. Motherhood is no picnic. It has challenges every day that test our strength and stamina. It is the one relationship (or in my case nine relationships) that is pretty much all me making sacrifices and all the other person taking what I have to give. Because of this distinction, we can sometimes feel like it's not okay to admit that we need to make some changes. We think we are supposed to just take whatever is thrown at us and not complain about it.

But recognizing a problem is not complaining. You must be willing to see it before you can change it. And if you are going to bed at night dreading tomorrow, then you need to make some changes and fast. Kid problems can be complicated and they are always shifting and changing paths, so just jump in and get started and let the pathway take you where you need to go.

ASSESS: If you're ready, let's do this thing. When assessing a situation, you may need to get a pen and paper. Sometimes a problem has multiple causes and even more possible solutions.

I can't possibly name every kid problem here. There are typical ones, such as tantrums and fevers; some that are a little outside of normal, such as autism or ADD; and others that morph from one problem to another, such as lying or getting in trouble at school. There are so many variations that, suffice it to say, we *all* deal with something with our children. Sometimes it's because of the child's own sin nature and tendencies, and other times it starts with an issue completely outside of all of us.

Look carefully at every angle of your problem. You will be working on your responses and reactions to what your kids do, so this is an exercise in being aware of their actions. Sometimes you may not know if it's a big issue or a small issue (things such as food, schoolwork, and focus could go either way). Pay attention to what your instincts tell you. (A mother's instincts are strong—like Jedi powers!) Then take a step back and view it as if it were someone else's problem. What if a friend were asking for your advice on how she should react; what would you say?

Try to find the root of the problem. Look at it from a deeper perspective. Does this issue (either in you or in your child) stem from selfishness? Self-control? Stubbornness? If you can see the root, then it is easy to apply the Bible to your situation. Which leads me to the next step.

LEARN: At no time in your life will this ever be so valuable. You are exhausted, frustrated, and not sure if you are causing permanent damage to another human being. Let me assure you, you probably are. Sorry, but if it makes you feel better, every other mom is too.

There are no perfect parents and there are no perfect kids. All of my kids will probably need therapy someday even if it's just because I moved the furniture around so much.

Knowing what God says is *so* valuable when you're actively parenting your children. And here's a tip that seems to get lost in the moments of adorableness: God's Word applies to your kids just as much as any adult. This means hurting others, lying, stealing, wanting what someone else has, etc. are still wrong even if you're three. The difference is that they are still learning this, so we give them much more room to get it wrong. We just correct them, give them a consequence to teach them, and share grace. Oh, God's amazing grace!

But it is wrong to be jealous no matter how old you are. We can only teach them that if we know what the Bible has to say about it. Of course we give them space to learn these things. There are times when kids can do what adults can't and it's perfectly fine. They can sing in the grocery store and wear tutus and walk right up to a stranger and ask to be picked up. There's nothing wrong with any of those things, but adults don't do them. We have a social understanding of what's acceptable and makes other people uncomfortable. But if it's something that the Bible says is wrong, then it's wrong for everyone. It's just that the consequences of these things when you're a kid are cushioned with lessons and hugs. Understanding this concept of right and wrong will help you know how to respond better to your child.

This is only one example of the brilliance in God's Word! When we are struggling to understand how to deal with a difficult situation, we can find wisdom in its pages.

And there are many wise people who have written brilliant books on the subject of parenting. Get some. I like an audiobook so I can listen while I am exercising or driving. Find ways to learn, and always be improving your outlook.

Account: This would be the toughest one to measure because it is ever changing. Just when you get Susie to go on the potty, she starts to run from you in the parking lot. You finally taught Johnny to read, and all of a sudden he can't stop gagging over everything you feed him. Don't stop and rest, because another trial is waiting right around the corner.

This, my friend, is called maturity and growth. Each time your children face a new struggle, it is actually just them learning something now that will be a part of their foundation for life. You aren't really battling with green veggies; you are building a strong fortress for them to live in for the rest of their lives.

So how do we measure these motherhood imbalances? With love. Breadth and width and length of love. You'll need all that and more to get through this one. The truth is, the more you hold your children to the words of Scripture, even when it's hard, the more you love them. James Dobson calls it "tough love." The love of God's Word is your measuring tool when you're figuring out mom problems. It's patient, kind, does not envy or boast, is not arrogant or rude, does not insist on its own way, is not irritable or resentful, and does not rejoice at wrongdoing but rejoices with the truth (1 Cor. 13:4–6). This is what we look for to know if what we are doing is working or not.

NOTIFY: If you don't know what to do, ask a friend who has been through it and is a little ahead of you down the road. You may find some great nuggets of ideas in what someone else suggests. Take it apart and look at each aspect of their ideas without being defensive. It's so easy to feel hurt when someone makes recommendations about your mothering, so just listen with an open mind.

CHANGE: This is it. You can get some balance back in this area of your life. You may not be able to change your children or the problems they are having, but you can find it within yourself. You can get a handle on your reactions and make some positive changes.

The changes you make will have a ripple effect in your family. When they see you being more peaceful, that will rub off on them and they may start to change. Look at your goals, to be calmer or to get up earlier or to smile more. It takes only a few little changes to make a huge impact. I encourage you not to overwhelm yourself by trying to do something drastic. Start small and work your way up.

ENDURE: The kids are used to things the way they are and might not jump on your happy bandwagon. They will lose some of their control when you stop reacting to their whines, and they might revolt. Hold your ground, and do what you know is right. They will get the message, and you will be on the path to a happier family sooner than you think!

In *How to Ruin Your Child in Seven Easy Steps*, the authors made this point so beautifully:

To paraphrase, your children are likely to make the same mistakes you do. If you don't conquer lust, chances are your son won't either. If you fall victim to envy, your daughter probably will too. If you don't conquer a sin, don't expect them to overcome it either. Maybe that doesn't scare you, but it sure scares me!

But here's the positive side of the same truth: When you invest time in changing yourself—even a little bit—it gives you enormous leverage to influence change in your children.[4]

Having had so many children myself, with five already finished with school and doing their own thing in life, I want to say that it doesn't get easier. I expected motherhood to kind of coast once the kids were grown, but it doesn't work that way, and because I wish someone had told me that, I am telling you. Their problems when they are adults are much bigger and harder to watch. It is not easy to know when to help and when to stay back and leave it alone. Do you give advice? Do you let them move back in? Do you rush to their side when they fall? There are no concrete answers but to know the Word of God, spend gobs of time with Him, and pray. Then pray some more.

On the flip side, their successes are so amazing and it's a delight to watch them move into adulthood. I have learned more from my grown kids than I ever expected, and it's been one of the greatest blessings of my life.

Motherhood is a rush from beginning to end—even though there are times in the toddler years when you're playing with blocks and think you will die of boredom—and I wouldn't have it any other way.

ASSIGNMENT

This is simple. Write down ten things about each of your children that you admire. Then focus on those areas and build them up. Every day mention one of these things to them and tell them how good they are at that and ask if there's a way you can help them in that area. When they walk into the room, do something to let them know you're glad they're there before you give an instruction or critique.

As a homeschool mom, this is especially challenging. Part of my relationship with my kids is to correct their schoolwork. I find that if I make comments on what they did right, or worked extra hard on, it helps them to hear when I make corrections. My list of ten things really helps in this as well. If I am correcting a high school essay, I can use my list and remark on that. "Wow! You really are so creative! That is one of your most amazing gifts and I love how you tap into that in this paper. Thanks for giving that some extra effort! In creativity you get an A. However, this is a history assignment and all of your facts are actually wrong, so let's try again. Keep the creativity but make sure that you use the correct dates and names."

HOME SWEET HOME

He who dwells in the shelter of the Most High
will abide in the shadow of the Almighty.

Psalm 91:1

THE BATHROOM WINDOW

In our house we have a girls' bathroom and a boys' bathroom. The boys' bathroom has an exterior door with a window in it. As you can imagine, this window stays pretty dirty. The bathroom itself is a battle of my endurance; some days I lose, and some days I put on the armor and head in to see what grime I need to chip away at in there.

One morning I had had enough of the dirty window. It's double paned, and there is no access to the area between the panes of glass. I will never understand how, but they had somehow gotten dirt, actual dirt, in between these two pieces of glass, and on this day I was *going to deal with it.*

I told my husband, James, "Today is the last day I am going to look at that big blob of brown on the boys' bathroom window. If it takes me all day, I *will* go to sleep tonight with that window clean."

He got that look in his eye, the way Ricky looked at Lucy when she told him one of her harebrained ideas. He suggested I wait and let him look at it over the weekend.

No way. I was perfectly capable of cleaning one window.

He kept saying things like, "Lisa, you know how you are; you break things."

What? What had I broken besides the oven door? Oh, and the front step. And maybe a few small things that didn't matter at all. I was determined, and I promised him that I would stop if I felt like I was doing anything that could potentially break the window.

So after I settled the kids into their schoolwork and got my other morning jobs done, I gathered my equipment together and headed for the boys' bathroom. In addition to the usual glass-cleaning supplies, I had screwdrivers, pliers, an X-Acto knife, and a small hammer. I had done a few quick inspections and at easy glance couldn't find a way into that window. But if the dirt got in there, so could I.

I started exploring the teeny plastic trim around the window and opened the door to see if it came apart on the side. I knew I could try to pry off the trim, but that would mean breaking it, and I was not sure I could easily replace it. So I opted to check everything I could before I did that. Eventually, using one of the boys' magnifying glasses, I noticed little plugs in the plastic trim. So I made the executive decision to use the X-Acto knife to dig out a plug. Lo and behold, behind the nearly invisible plug was a teeny screw. Okay, there you go! I proceeded to find the rest of the plastic plugs and dig them out too.

When they were all out, I used a small screwdriver to take out the screws, and with one easy move the window, the *whole* window, came out of the door. Mkay. Now I had another problem. I got the window out, but I still couldn't get to the layer between.

I carried the window to my bed, set it down carefully, and started fiddling around with it, hoping that I could quickly get the window apart before my husband noticed the giant hole in the door (he worked in an office at home). Finally, after about an hour and lots of little screws and door-window pieces in a pile on my bed, I separated the panes and cleaned them.

It took me about forty-five more minutes, but eventually I reassembled the window and put it back in the door. Yes, the trim now had little holes in it, but I would fix that later with caulk and paint. My motto: "Caulk fixes everything."

That evening I proudly escorted my husband into the bathroom to show him the beautifully cleaned window. He was impressed (except for the trim holes) and patted me on the back. Then he opened the door to look at the outside and—*crash!*—the inside panes fell out of the door and shattered all over the bathroom floor.

Talk about surprised! We both just stood there like we were in a TV sitcom.

James looked at me and smiled. "Well, at least now we can keep the window clean more easily."

Lemons, meet lemonade.

NOT BEVERLY HILLS

Cleaning windows, doing laundry, and organizing are just small parts of the big job of creating and maintaining a home. As a child of the '70s, I grew up watching *The Beverly Hillbillies*. That mansion with the marble foyer and cement pond was impressive.

But what you learn from that show is that no matter what you are surrounded by, you make it your own. The Clampetts still cooked over a fire in a cast-iron pot and made their own lye soap. And Granny wasn't trading her moonshine for a wine cellar.

We definitely do not live in a Beverly Hills mansion. In fact, we live out in the country. I've lived in tiny houses, old houses, and outdated houses; it's not about what you start with but what you make it. You make your house a home by how you arrange it, how you keep it, and how you spend your time there. You have choices, even when it gets overwhelming. In my house almost every stick of furniture was either a hand-me-down or from a flea market. I chose very few of the pieces. I just took what I could get. Then I, in the words of Disney, reimagined it to make it my own. A little paint and some throw pillows go a *long* way. I will even cut something up and make it into something else.

Maybe your style is more sleek and less, um, trash inspired than mine. I love sleek and contemporary. It's my alter ego. I could definitely enjoy a room with simple furnishings and very few accessories. You can do smooth surfaces and simple decor with people's leftovers just as easily as the shabby country look of my house. Of course, I live in the shabby country so it's easy for me to decide a style. You don't have to be creative to find a look that you like. If you struggle with this, ask a friend to help! I would trade furniture-arranging time for cooking lessons anytime.

But your home isn't just style; it's practical life. I often say that because there are so many people in our house and we homeschool, which means we are *always* home and we *use* every inch of our space.

I have to make a practical use out of everything. If I can make something into storage or workspace, I will. IKEA, by the way, which I refer to on my blog as "the mothership," is great for this kind of thing. They are masters of small spaces with large usefulness.

Your home is also the reflection of your lifestyle. Are you messy? Why? Is it a time issue, or do you just not care, or are you too overwhelmed to know where to start? Do you have too much stuff? Are toys overtaking your house until eventually you are pretty sure you will turn into plastic and require batteries? What are your life challenges that have converted into home challenges? We all have them.

Lastly, your home is your place of rest. Can you rest there? Are you able to think clearly and relax? If not, let's figure out how to fix that.

WHO BUILT YOUR HOUSE?

"By wisdom a house is built, and by understanding it is established; by knowledge the rooms are filled with all precious and pleasant riches" (Prov. 24:3–4).

Do you believe that everything you have is a gift from God? I can forget that sometimes and be all like "Hey that's *mine*!" and start to become a hoarder; or worse, I throw it all out in frustration with no thought for what I will need later on (some of this can be covered in the "Moods" chapter).

Your home, no matter if it's a brick house or an apartment or a room in your parents' house or a condo in the big city, was built by

God and is a gift to you. Even if you actually built it yourself, He gave you the knowledge, the materials, the strength, and the inspiration to do it. He is the giver of all things, and we are wise to remember that as we look at our mansion and see how we can find balance.

Many times in the Bible, God uses the word *cornerstone* as a picture of Christ in our lives. But what is a cornerstone? Webster's 1828 says it is "the stone which lies at the corner of two walls and unites them." God was using construction terms to describe Christ's role in our lives—He is the first and most important piece of our foundation, and everything else should be built on that or it will fall apart.

Talk about a great picture of balance! Sometimes all we need to do is just go back to the cornerstone and build from there. In other words, just keep your eyes on Jesus! Everything else is additional.

LIVING THE DREAM

I live in a ninety-three-year-old farmhouse that we have added on to in several directions. It came with one small closet and no insulation. We have made the best of it and even have come to enjoy the freezing winters and sweaty summer afternoons in the living room. For some there's a fantasy of buying an old farmhouse and fixing it up and adding a huge front porch, raising chickens, and living the dream. Well, I don't want to kill your dreams, but I have that and it's not easy. The house is always needing repair, the chickens and goats are a lot of work (and they stink), and there's never enough money to do what needs to be done. And it's dirty. Always dirty. But the porch, I'm not gonna lie, is pretty fantastic.

I tell you this not to brag (believe me, come for a visit; it's nothing to brag about) but to tell you that we worked *hard* for this. It was one teeny step at a time and a lot of prayer. God led us, very slowly, to this place and I plan to die here, which if we can't afford to redo the insulation soon, might happen this summer. Whatever your dream for a home is, don't give it up!

Before this, we lived in neighborhoods. We adapted our homes to our needs and I went through a lot of paint. When we rented, I hung fabric over the walls or used painted boards to cover places I couldn't change. Whatever your situation or whatever lemon you are living in, you can find lemonade there somewhere!

What if you had to live where you are forever? Could you make it work for you? Could you find peace? If not, then we need to work on some attitudes. When you're feeling discontent about where you live, spend a few minutes focusing on someone else, like the person with no home at all. Or the hut in Africa made of hay and dirt. Now, are you feeling better about where you live?

My friend Myquillyn Smith ("The Nester") has a beautiful book called *The Nesting Place*. In addition to providing gorgeous photos in the book, she encourages us to love where we live: "Home. A place of rest while we are on this earth. A safe place for our children. A place to love and be loved. A place that is beautiful. A haven. With enough money, anybody can create a pretty house. But it takes intention to create a home."[1]

You, believe it or not, are already living the dream. You have a roof and stuff (if you're like me, lots of stuff you don't need!) and ideas and a desire to improve. You have everything you need, and what you don't have God knows about and will give it to you when the time is best for you.

We need to dismiss the idea that we have to own Pinterest-worthy homes before we can be happy. You can always improve and have lists of things to change, but joy is ready for you right now and it is not dependent on your surroundings. Don't believe the lie that it will make you happy anyway. My home has been in magazines and it's all over Pinterest, and I have plenty of miserable days.

One afternoon a stranger knocked on my door. When I opened it, she said immediately, "I'm sorry to bother you, but I drive past your house every day and it's so cozy that I just had to get closer. So I pulled up your driveway and I see how peaceful it is and I just couldn't stop from knocking on your door to meet you. Your home is perfect. You must have a perfect life."

Just moments before, I had been mopping up water in my utility room from a leak in the water heater while the kids ran around doing who knows what. I had a list on my fridge of a hundred things I wanted to change about my house with dollar and time amounts next to each. My bedroom was a disaster because it had become a dumping ground from cleaning out the kids' home-school books, and I had no idea where to put the stuff we didn't use. Perfect life? Hardly.

If we place importance on the look of our home and ignore the people in it (or worse, make them feel pressured to keep up the facade), then we have completely missed the purpose of home. It is for living. As we go through the BALANCE system, be sure we are connecting with the true meaning of a well-balanced home.

THE PILES

Oh my word, the piles. It seems that just as I clear out one, another pops up somewhere else. Laundry piles and paper piles and shoe piles and toy piles and old clothes and dishes and books. Or, wait, books are technically stacks, not piles. And I have stacks too; besides books I've got cup stacks and folded towel stacks and I even have stacks of empty egg cartons because we have chickens and people give me their old egg cartons. So what do we do with all of these piles and stacks?

Here's the thing. If I don't have a place to put it, I don't keep it. I decide to either toss out the egg cartons or get rid of some things in a kitchen cabinet that I don't use and put the cartons there. It might take me awhile, but I do eventually put the piles away.

If you have a problem with piles and stacks, here are a few tips:

1. Start with one pile. Have laser focus on that one and don't think about any other messes around the house. Give yourself a time limit for putting away everything in that pile (from a day to a week).

2. If you are using the stuff in the pile all the time, maybe you need to get rid of some things buried in the cabinet to make room for it. It's not always the stuff in the pile that needs to be discarded, but what you never use.

3. Declare one surface to remain clear. I never, ever use a table or countertop for gathering clutter.

These are spaces we need to work or eat or cook or, hold on to your hat, just stay clean. If you have every flat surface in your house cluttered with little piles, pick one and clean it off. Then let the family know that anything sitting there at the end of the day will be confiscated and not returned until the surface stays clear for a week.

4. Some things you just need to get brutal about. Magazines, promotional cups, craft supplies, old calendars, ketchup packets (my husband keeps these—do not get me started), used gift bags, stained shirts; need I go on? These things need to go away and make room for fresh, useful things in your life. Or better yet, have a place with nothing in it.

5. Watch an episode of *Hoarders*. That will make me clean up my piles so fast my family's heads will spin.

Crystal Paine is a master of this. Her book *Say Goodbye to Survival Mode* says, "You know one sure fire way to add more time and order to your life? Get rid of excess stuff. I talked about this before, but I'll say it again. I truly believe that the less you have, the less time you spend on upkeep, maintenance, and cleaning. Either you control the clutter or the clutter will control you."[2]

Clutter is a sign that your home time is out of balance. If you're just setting things down and they're still sitting there a month later, you need to make some changes.

GIRL, YOU HAVE NO IDEA!

Some of you are thinking, *I wish I just had a few piles of junk to deal with. My whole house is a mess beyond help.* I know, it gets to be so daunting that you feel like you are doomed to live in the Pit of Despair for the rest of your life. You're not a natural cleaner, you don't care if it's messy, you can't keep it clean because your family won't help, you're never home, you don't know where to start, all good moms have messy houses—the excuses outnumber the stars in the sky.

If you can't find things, don't entertain, are embarrassed when people come over, can't find a surface to set things down on, or wish your home was different, then you are out of balance and it's time to get up and do something about it.

I will admit; I tend toward the overly tidy and not messy, but I know I am in the minority. I have friends who won't have me over because their houses are messy. Really? Either let me see it (and I don't care, by the way) or clean it up. Are you going to let *stuff* keep you from building a relationship with someone? If you want to hide the mess, then you are keeping people from knowing the real you. Life's too short to be embarrassed by where you live.

Straightening up is telling yourself and your family that you are worth the extra effort. Your home, as a gift, is worth keeping clean to a standard that you can set for yourself. Don't compare yourself to others; compare yourself to what you want to be.

BALANCE

BEGIN: Let's do this thing. Jump in. Choose a pile or a room to paint or a closet to clean, and motivate yourself to do it.

ASSESS: So what is the problem? Where have you lost the battle? Do you have visions for your decor that you feel defeated about because you don't have money? Is the closet such a mess that you don't know where your winter coat is? Do your kids have so many toys that you could open your own Toys "R" Us?

Take a look around you right now (if you're at home of course). What is right in your line of sight that you'd like to change? What can you do with what you have right now? Where do you need help?

I love to make lists. I write down to-do lists and home-repair lists and wish lists and school lists and blog-idea lists—I am a list-aholic. But the lists actually *do* help. Especially when we start looking around the house at things that we need to change so our lives can run more smoothly or be more peaceful.

Once you've seen what you would like to change, divide the list into some things you could do in the next few weeks to design a longer project. You can't make a huge change all at once. If you tried, it would go right back as soon as you sat down from exhaustion.

LEARN: I was once so stumped about how to arrange the furniture in a very oddly shaped living room we had that I hired a designer to come over and help me. She didn't normally work on a onetime-only basis, but I think my crying in her office while nursing a baby and juggling a toddler made her feel sorry for me. I took the opportunity while she was at my house to pick her brain about everything. I learned about books and community classes and concepts of design and where she had been educated. Eventually she did help me find a workable furniture configuration, but the best part was all the knowledge I got from her.

I have friends who are great at cleaning or organizing or decorating or managing a daily schedule. I ask for their advice, lean in, and listen. There are books and HGTV shows and blogs. There are many ways to learn!

The Bible does have things to say about the value of keeping a home. But even more, it talks about how we are supposed to live. We are to be pure and holy, and we are to walk carefully and make the best use of our time. Part of being thankful for the gifts God has given you means not neglecting them or tossing them in a corner.

I am praying that while you read through this chapter you will see the ways your home is a reflection of other areas in your heart, both bad and good. There are areas in your home where you are doing a great job! If not, then stop right now and go wash the dishes and clean the sink. It's a start. Do it every day—that one thing until it becomes easy—then do something else. And watch your life begin to have small victories too.

ACCOUNT: It's pretty easy to tell if what you're doing is working. How long has it been since you couldn't find your keys? Do you run out of clean underwear frequently? How much time are you spending on cleaning, and are your kids helping?

We can use our lists as measurements. If you looked around and wrote down, "Get the kids to put away their backpacks," then that's an easy way to measure if what you are trying is working. How many days this week did they follow your new plan? If they didn't put them away most of the time, try something else.

If you wanted to build shelves in the playroom, that may take some time, but have you done anything toward it? Bought plans or shopped for the best prices or looked for scrap-shelf ideas? Keep moving in the direction of your goals and you'll be doing fine!

NOTIFY: You may live in your house alone (or with people who don't help), but you are not alone in your dream of having a balanced home. All of us have dreams of what we want our homes to be like. Me, I want my own closet to stay tidy, but for some reason it fights me. No matter how much I straighten it, there always seems to be at least one messy spot (and it's usually the floor).

A neat home will look different to me than it does to you. I might want my clothes hung in order of color and you might just be glad they're on hangers. It doesn't matter. Whatever your standard is, you need help living up to it. Ask for help. (This is a great time to get the kids involved in keeping the house clean and tidy.) Don't try to make big changes without being open and honest with the people in your life.

If you share your goals with your husband, he will be able to lovingly help you stay on target. After all, he lives there! But don't expect him to automatically jump in and make his goals match with yours. This isn't a way to force him to do the dishes more often or keep his clothes off the floor. This is you telling him your goal and asking him to help advise you when you're struggling. Be careful not to use this as an excuse to manipulate him to do what you want. If you can keep the focus on your vision for yourself and just let him be a partner, it can be a great help!

I used to be leery of telling my husband about my goals because I had nowhere to hide when I slipped up. If you're feeling that way, talk to your husband about it. If you only want his advice when you ask for it, let him know that. Or if you want to just check in about it once a week while you're figuring things out, tell him. Be honest about your needs or it could put a strain on your relationship.

One warning: do *not* ask your kids to hold you accountable. You can tell them what you are trying to do and they will likely be annoying little reminders of how you're doing. But don't give them the responsibility of making sure you are doing what you have said. It is not healthy for your child to think he has to keep you in line. That is not God's design for your relationship.

CHANGE: Changes are hard, especially when we are overwhelmed and everything else in life seems more important. But the rooms you live in, the places you are breathing and sleeping and loving and eating in are important. They are making a huge contribution to your success, and frankly, they are an easy place to make changes.

Right this second, as I am writing this for you, I am making changes. I work in my bedroom and we have had lots of houseguests recently, so things got out of balance. It happens. So I spent ten minutes going around my bedroom putting things away, and what belongs somewhere else I put in a laundry basket by the door. Then I called my twelve-year-old to come help, and while I am writing, he is picking up one thing at a time from the basket, and if he doesn't know where it goes, he asks me. In a few minutes the bedroom will be a calmer place and I will be able to focus more on my work.

Barbara Reich, author of *Secrets of an Organized Mom*, said, "Organizing is incredibly valuable. It's remarkable, the degree to which our messes can hold us back—and it's amazing how much freedom, peace of mind, and confidence we can achieve once we confront and eliminate clutter and piles."[3]

How can you creatively make a solid plan for change? If your need is to empty the junk drawer (or drawers) and organize their contents, do one drawer at a time each week. If you need to do a bigger job, section it off and make deadlines. Do you need to get rid of things? Pick one a week and toss it or take it to the nearest charity shop. By the end of the year you will have fifty-two things gone. You might even start a movement!

ENDURE: Your home didn't get messy or out of balance in a week and it won't get to be the way you want it in a short time. You may even be able to make some big changes quickly, but then it still needs constant maintenance. You know how nice it is when you have a party and the next day the house is all clean and there's left-over party food in the fridge? Then a week later you're right back to barely keeping the dishes clean? That's life, my friend. Maintaining and caring for a home is an unending task. But we can do things to make it a lot easier and move toward a balance of being able to find what we need and not having to dig for a place to sit.

Be patient with yourself. You'll do better some weeks than others. The key is to keep moving in the direction of a better lifestyle, not perfection.

JUST BE *YOU*

Your home reflects you. Looking on Pinterest is great for ideas, but don't get dragged down by your lack of ability to make your room look like that blogger's. If you aren't as creative with furniture arranging, ask a friend to come over and help. Trade her for something you're good at, and don't tell me you have nothing to offer her. There's always a way to bless someone. Offer to babysit her kids for the afternoon or make their dinner. If someone offered to trade me coming to their house to help them decorate in exchange for them organizing my receipts for the past month, I would jump on it!

Your home doesn't have to be a designer showcase to reflect your personality. In fact, it can't! That just reflects the designer who picked out all the furniture and ordered the drapes. Instead, let your home be a reflection of the Designer, the One who made you and gave you this place to live. While you're deciding how to get your home in balance, when to clean, what color to paint, where to put the kids' artwork, and whether to keep that kitchen gadget you wanted so badly but have never used, stop and think about what is honoring to God. Could someone else use that gadget more? Do the kids really need all their toys? Is there a paint color that makes you feel at peace? Could cleaning the house become an act of worship?

I am excited for you to take these steps toward finding balance in your mansion. I have so much faith in you!

ASSIGNMENT

Think of five things you do well around your house. Even if it's something small, such as "I am great at replacing the toilet paper roll." Write down those five things and stick the list to your mirror or wherever you put inspiration (if you don't have a place, find one; I use the back of my closet door). Now each day when you see the list, thank God for those gifts. Each of those is one area where you shine, and I can promise you there are people who struggle with it. Gratitude is a game changer when you're trying to find balance.

GETTING OUT OF THE HOUSE

As each has received a gift, use it to serve one another,
as good stewards of God's varied grace.

1 Peter 4:10

THE GOLDEN GATE BRIDGE

I travel about once a month for business. It's usually to speak at a conference, but occasionally I go to meet a blog sponsor who hires me to promote their business. One year I went to San Francisco to meet a sponsor in person and see their headquarters. It was a wonderful trip and I decided on the last morning that I would take advantage of the opportunity to mark something off my bucket list. I wanted to go for a run across the Golden Gate Bridge.

I talked to my hotel concierge and he told me that if I took a taxi out there around 6:00 a.m., then I could easily catch another one to get back when I was ready. I believe his exact words were, "Oh sure! There are taxis there all the time!"

So I took the cab, had my glorious run, and around 7:30 walked back from the bridge out to the street to catch a taxi. The place was completely deserted. I picked up my phone to call for a cab, and yep, you guessed it, the battery was dead. Too many selfies on the bridge, I guess.

I felt panicked because I had to catch a plane around lunch-time. Soon a bus came around the corner and I thought, *I'll just hop on there and figure out what to do next.* Of course, I had no idea how buses worked. I did have a credit card with me, but I discovered within seconds of the door closing behind me and the bus taking off that they don't take credit, only cash. Two dollars. The driver started screaming at me in some foreign language and I was near tears when a passenger started calling out for people to help. They all pulled out change from their pockets until I had the two dollars.

After giving the driver the money, I took a seat, not sure what to do next. I asked a man how to get to Union Square, which was across the street from my hotel. He told me I would have to change buses at least once. Great. I had no cash.

I rode for many stops until the driver started pointing at me and yelling for me to get off. A woman who seemed to understand him told me that he said this was my stop and to change buses for Union Square. Okay, off I got and then thought, *Lord, what do I do?*

I found a map of the bus system near a bench and studied it, wondering if I could possibly walk the rest of the way. But it was about fifty blocks, up and down hills and through some potentially questionable neighborhoods. I decided to stand at the next bus stop and hope to figure out the money thing, but keep my eye out for a taxi as well.

The area was pretty residential and I never saw a single taxi. So much for that idea. As I stood there, I noticed an older Asian couple who had been sitting on the bus near me before. I smiled at them and they gruffly turned away, probably embarrassed to be seen with the woman who was waiting for a bus with no money. After about fifteen minutes several more people had gathered, and half an hour later I could hear them all discussing why it might be taking so long for the buses to come.

Then a bus came around the corner but was completely full. It didn't even stop. Seven or eight minutes later, another full bus zoomed by, and fifteen minutes after that, another. I was really starting to panic! Eventually a bus came that had enough room to let us all on and I waited until the last because I was going to have to explain to the driver that I had no money. But just as the Asian man passed me to board the bus, he poked me on the elbow and thrust two dollars into my hand. I was never so grateful for anything. I tried to thank him, but he had already hurried onto the bus.

As I got on, I stood by the driver, who was a very large sixty-three-year-old black man (I know his age because he told me, along with everything else about his life). With desperation in my voice I said to him, "I really need to get to Union Square. Does this bus go there?"

I braced myself for the yelling, but he just laughed and told me to stick with him and he would get me where I needed to go. "Stand right here, little lady, and I will take good care of you."

I spent the next half hour listening to him talk about the bus drivers' strike that morning and that only a handful of drivers were working. He told me all about how he was asleep when he got the call and how his wife was mad because she had plans for him that day to go see their granddaughter. (For the record, he has eleven grandchildren.)

Another woman on the bus gave me her business card and told me to call her if I needed any more help while I was in the city. We are now Facebook friends. I also got to hear the story of a homeless man who this driver allows to ride free all day so he has a place to rest. Different people on the bus handed the homeless man food they had brought for him as they boarded. He even returned a Tupperware container to one woman.

Finally, two hours and forty-five minutes after I had been standing at the Golden Gate Bridge, I was back at my hotel. Thankfully, I still had time to catch my flight. I would have never, ever planned that crazy morning in San Francisco, but what an incredible experience! I got to meet new people and see sights I will never have the opportunity to see again. Even now I could describe the bus stop where I stood for an hour waiting and the Asian man's jacket and the way it felt to have a bus full of strangers pulling their change together for me.

And overall, I will always remember that run across the Golden Gate Bridge. I remember thinking at the time, *This is amazing! I wonder what my next adventure will be!* I just had no idea it was minutes away.

LEAVING THE HOUSE

In this chapter I am going to cover anything we do outside of our homes, from volunteering to jobs to church to kids' activities.

Leaving the home is a big deal, even though we do it all the time and some of us several times a day. Our time is valuable, no matter who you are. Between grocery shopping and working extra jobs and driving kids to soccer and being at church on Wednesday, we can feel as though we hardly have time to breathe! Outside responsibilities and commitments can very quickly get out of balance and before you know it you haven't had dinner as a family in over a month and you haven't spent any time alone with God.

I think of everything I do outside my home as a ministry. If I am traveling for work, I look at it as a time to bless the people I work with. If I am driving kids to an activity, I am serving their needs. When I go to the grocery store, I am providing food and toilet paper for my family. Thinking of everything we do outside of our home as our ministry adapts an attitude of service to our choices. Anything that pulls us from family and home must be worth the time away. It must perform a service to someone else, or a group. Whether you get paid can't be the only criterion for deciding if you should accept an opportunity. Use the balance method to decide if it fits other needs you have, like family time, travel distance, etc. Or if you've been offered a leadership role in your child's sports league, you have many things to consider besides your qualifications for the job. This chapter is about how we make our choices and how we spend our time and efforts.

In my life, even though I am *inside* my home, I am still doing outside ministry because I am writing or blogging or working on my essential-oils business. I am there, but not. I actually have "office hours" so my kids know that they need to leave me alone during certain time frames. I get them all settled with what they are supposed to be doing, make a few lists of tasks or schoolwork for them, then get to my work. I consider myself a work-at-home mom. It's not easy to juggle home and work at the same time. Most days get interrupted with questions or accidents or some kind of struggle the kids are having. I just stop and deal with it. Life isn't smooth, my friend. Don't be disappointed when your days are disrupted by your family; just handle their needs and keep going.

I have many friends who work outside of the home, both full time and part time. It's not easy! The idea that we can have it all is bunk. But we can have joy in all areas. That's where finding balance comes in.

WHY DO WE DO IT?

Our reasons for spending time away from home are as numerous as the stars in the sky. It's not what you do or why you do it, but making sure you are finding a proper balance is what I want to focus on. But I have to say for the record, you should pray about your service and do it as unto the Lord and not because someone else is doing it. *You must* be *you* and not anyone else!

In terms of jobs, it may also be necessary for your family's well-being that you bring in an income. I encourage you to be on the same page with your husband about this; it makes life rough when you disagree about something that takes you away from your family regularly. If you do need to have a job, whether it is inside or outside of the home, make sure you have determined what will work for your family and what won't. Is it better for you to work evenings only? Are you able to distribute the household responsibilities? Does the job you have move you toward a goal, even if not financially? There are numerous other worthwhile goals, like doing community service, volunteering at church, serving on a nonprofit board, helping those in need, feeding a sick neighbor, teaching a Bible study, coaching a children's sports team, and many, many more!

It could be that you feel deeply called to children's ministry at church or to be the homeroom mom in your child's class. Maybe you have a gift for organization or music or you just love folding papers and stuffing them in envelopes. Try to find ways to use those gifts while you are spending time outside the home. It can be a beautiful thing if you can tap into your gifts when you're away from home. You're happy, you're doing great work, others are blessed, and all of that is a benefit to your family.

One of my favorite books I read recently is *Essentialism* by Greg McKeown. He talks about eliminating everything that is not essential and making room for what you are supposed to be doing:

> The way of the Essentialist means living by design, not by default. Instead of making choices reactively, the Essentialist deliberately distinguishes the vital few from the trivial many, eliminates the nonessentials, and then removes obstacles so the essential things have clear, smooth passage. In other words, essentialism is a disciplined, systematic

approach for determining where our highest point of contribution lies, then making execution of those things almost effortless.[1]

We must look at each decision for how we spend our extra time carefully and make sure it fits with our personal values and goals. Just because an opportunity pops up doesn't make it the best thing to do. Be sure you know why you are doing any activity, and don't be afraid to let someone down. It is necessary sometimes.

For all of the whys, there are just as many why nots. Be careful how you spend your time outside of the home. God said in Psalm 84:11, "For the LORD God is a sun and shield; the LORD bestows favor and honor. No good thing does he withhold from those who walk uprightly." In other words, it's your walk He is concerned with more than what specific ministry you're doing.

JUST SAY NO

I used to have a bad habit of filling every space of time in my day. I didn't want to waste a second just sitting in the swing or feeling the breeze. I could be getting more done if I made my list longer and tried to do four things at once. This is how I became known as the mom who burns dinner every night. I'd put the bread in the oven … Oh, look, I have twenty-five minutes to go do something else before the bread is ready. I'll put the toys away. Oh, look, there's that shoe I was trying to find yesterday; I've got time to go put that where it belongs. Oh, look, the closet is messy; I'll just straighten it a little—what's that smell coming from the kitchen? Burning bread.

Now, I just let myself linger. I might use the time to wipe down the kitchen, but I don't get lost in jobs all over the house. I will use the in-between time of my day to talk to my kids and ask about their lives. I might play some music or update my to-do list. But I have gotten to know myself, and I no longer wander off from a task with the idea that I can get more done. I don't even check Facebook—whoa!

I recommend having a "time budget." Sit down with your family and decide how much time you can spend on ministry (remember, this is anything from work to service) and still have a healthy family. Once you have determined that, keep the time you spend on outside activities within this limit. It's the same with money; you only have so much. I'd donate money to every need that crossed my path if I didn't have a set amount to give that our family has agreed on. Doing this with your time is a great measuring tool for knowing when to say no. Or if you say yes, but your time allowance is filled, then you have to let something else go.

Saying no and leaving breathing room is hard in our go-go-go society. We convince ourselves and others that we need to be busy all the time. In fact, we sell the idea that being busy is good and having free time is bad. Don't believe it, friend! It is good to have space in your schedule.

Another quote from *Essentialism* says this:

Play, which I would define as anything we do simply for the joy of doing it rather than as a means to an end—whether it's flying a kite or listening to music or throwing a baseball—might seem like a nonessential activity. Often it is treated that way. But in fact play *is* essential in many ways. Stuart Brown, the founder of the National Institute for Play, has studied what are called the play histories of some six thousand individuals and has concluded that play has the power to significantly improve everything from personal health to relationships to education to organizations' ability to innovate.[2]

I am not a minimalist, okay? I like having an active life the same way I like surrounding myself with trinkets that have no usefulness. For organizing activities, I divide them into essentials and nonessentials. I don't have any other columns. If I can't tell which one it is, then it's nonessential. Bam! When considering activities outside of the home, I have very few essentials.

Time away from home can get out of balance very quickly. One day I will look at my calendar for the next week and it's wide open. Then before I know it, I have crammed it full of activities. And when people find out you are willing to serve, they will ask for more and more. Your time is of great value; don't underestimate your worth in this area. If you're saying yes to every request that comes along, then you are not making wise choices and honoring the jobs God already gave you. Every time someone asks you for help or offers you a great opportunity doesn't mean it is God's will for you. Saying no is a powerful art.

DO YOU RECOGNIZE A GIFT WHEN YOU SEE IT?

You're awake in the middle of the night to feed the baby. She cries and you pick her up, slump into the soft chair, and begin feeding. How do you think of this time? It can be a burden that you kind of resent, wishing for it to end. Or it can be a precious few uninterrupted moments with your baby who will be too big for this before you know it. She will never remember; it is a mom gift.

Every opportunity can be seen in different ways. Your neighbor needs help with his trash cans, again. Do you see it as a blessing or a curse? You have to work a few extra hours this week; can that be seen as a gift to you from God even if it's not what you want to be doing? Of course it can! Look at every opportunity as a gift even if it feels like a burden. Even if you aren't going to use the opportunity, you can gain something from the experience of responding to it. Telling someone no is a craft that takes practice.

OKAY, IT'S A BEAUTIFUL GIFT, BUT I'M TIRED

Sometimes I wonder if I make it sound like I am in a good mood all the time. I talk about seeing service as a gift and rocking my baby and loving my friends and, oh, such a good life I have. Don't be fooled! I am not going to write about all the times I forgot to be glad and cried all the way through making lunch because I was too tired from trying to get a seven-year-old to understand long division. There are days when the fatigue of mothering and wife-ing takes its toll.

I once was so tired that I literally told the kids we were having a breakfast picnic on the living room floor because I wanted to take a nap on the couch while they ate. Weariness is no joke. It can make getting through simple tasks seem enormously difficult!

This is when you will be so glad you left space in your sched-ule for downtime. Leaving space doesn't mean your life is empty. Evaluating everything and making wise choices may mean you spend a year not doing much outside of the home. If you have a new baby or a child who has medical needs or a husband in a high-stress job, you have my permission to take some time *off*. Give notice to the committees and leadership roles, and take a break. If no one else can fill that role, then maybe it doesn't need to be filled.

Moms need rest, but the American way tells us otherwise. Plant a garden if you feel the need to stay occupied (although this wouldn't be an option for me because I kill even plastic plants), but stay close to home and get some rest. Here's a clue: if you find yourself dreading the things you have to do tomorrow, feel-ing sleepy behind the wheel, needing coffee to stay awake in the afternoons, using the word *stress* more than once a day to describe yourself, then you need to eliminate some things.

A great book, *Boundaries: When to Say Yes, How to Say No to Take Control of Your Life* (how's that for a title—yes, please!) by Dr. Henry Cloud and Dr. John Townsend, tells us that we have to remember to take good care of ourselves by setting boundaries on our time: "A helpful way to understand setting limits is that our lives are a gift from God. Just as a store manager takes good care of a shop for the owner, we are to do the same with our souls. If a lack of boundaries causes us to mismanage the store, the owner has a right to be upset with us."[3]

You don't have to be doing everything all the time. In fact, you shouldn't!

SO MANY CHOICES, SO LITTLE TIME

One of the great things about life in this century is we have choices. Not too many years ago people didn't have nearly as many options. Even when I was a kid, there were only six channels on TV and three of those were iffy or in Spanish. One hundred years ago there were only a few kinds of cars and now we have thousands. People didn't get to decide how to spend their time; they had to work all day just to get food on the table, then clean it up. Laundry took half a day, they could own only a few articles of clothing, and to get anywhere took so much effort and time that they didn't go out more than once a week. Whether to do VBS wasn't a part of their lives.

Now we are left with so many choices, we are almost un-prepared to make these decisions. I have never had someone give me tips for managing ministry decisions, at least none that I remember. So how are we supposed to know what to do with our time, how to make extra time, or when to say no?

Finding balance in your ministry time is a matter of understanding your vision for your life and sticking to it. Sit down with your spouse and ask yourself the following questions, then have a discussion about your answers. Go deep, maybe over a few nights.

> 1. Where do you see yourself in five years? This is in regard to your home, your finances, your kids, health and fitness, church, etc.
> 2. What is your passion? Do you want to see change in an area like politics, community needs, schools, or even something small like how people are greeted at your monthly meetings?
> 3. What would your perfect day look like? This will help you see what it is you really want.

I love John Maxwell and his teachings! He wrote a book called *Wisdom from Women of the Bible* in which he said:

> God gives many skills and talents. He gives them to every human being into which He breathes life. Some of those talents are greater, some lesser. Some tap into your passion; some don't. Some lead you straight to your purpose; others lead you

> astray. You have to make choices. Just because
> you see something you *could* do does not auto-
> matically mean it is something you *should* do.
> Don't let the desire to do something you could do
> well prevent you from doing what's really best.[4]

This is a great help to me when I am wondering if I am supposed to say yes to something that doesn't feel quite right.

Once you have gone over your vision, keep in mind that this
isn't set in stone. You can tweak it, and you should definitely go
over it at least once a year to see if your vision has changed. But
it is a basic tool for you to use to help you make decisions, so you
want it to be something you plan to work with and not make huge
changes in it without careful consideration.

After your vision is created, let's use that as one of the ways
we measure our efforts to find balance in how we spend time away
from home. Are you getting closer to and fulfilling the vision, or
not? It's a question to be considered for each outside activity from
work to a trip to the beach.

LET'S BALANCE!

BEGIN: You already started by determining a vision. In addition
to that, I encourage you to write down everything you do outside
of the home from work to dinner with friends. Think about your
time budget, and determine if you want to add or eliminate any
extra activities.

Assess: You have your list. Now look it over objectively. Removing your attachment to your choices will help a lot in deciding what to keep and what to eliminate. As I said earlier, figure out what are essentials and what are not. I suggested writing two columns, essential and nonessential. This is the time to do that.

Now look at your list, evaluate each activity, and be brutal. If you aren't getting enough time at home or your finances are a mess or your kids are struggling, you need to eliminate some things and pronto.

Learn: What does the Bible have to say about how we spend our extra time? I love the words of Colossians 4:5–6: "Walk in wisdom toward outsiders, making the best use of the time. Let your speech always be gracious, seasoned with salt, so that you may know how you ought to answer each person." He helps direct us by telling us to make good use of our time with outsiders—how beautiful! I interpret that as saying I have only a limited time with them, which is a good help in knowing that I don't need to be spending every spare second on things outside of my home.

You could spend some time studying more verses on how to be wise, what salt is, being gracious, and how the Bible interprets itself. That is one of the best things about Scripture study: it gets richer and more alive the more you look!

Account: Determining how to measure your time away from family is not difficult. I already mentioned using your vision as a jumping-off point. Keep a watch on whether you are getting closer to those goals.

You can also set a limit on how much time you will spend away from the family with your time budget.

My friend Sara is very sacrificial when it comes to her time. She will bend over backward, feed the poor, host weddings, throw showers, and help with any church activity, and yet she serves on every board of every group she has ever been in as far as I know. Call her and ask for help, and she will drop everything. But over time, I have watched her figure out when to say no and when to accept. She has learned the hard way not to be taken advantage of and to guard her family time.

One way she does this is she and her family faithfully observe Sabbath. As one of her closest friends, I know to never invite her to anything on Sabbath because this is her commitment to God and her family. I deeply respect that she honors this, and it is so obvious how it helps her through the rest of the week. She lays every item of work aside for one day every week. It's beautiful!

I have been influenced by her to keep a set time each week for rest and family. We keep it casual: no electronics and no hard work. No matter how tempting it is, we leave the mess for the next day. It's hard for this OCD mama to do, but I do it. This is a great example of using a different way to measure. Maybe if you don't know *what* to say no to, you can establish *when* to say it.

Find a way to measure what is working for your family. If you are unable to get dinner on the table most nights because of your work, does this create problems? Then make a goal that within a month you will be making dinner twice a week with leftovers for the other nights. If you are exhausted every weekend so much that you're missing the enjoyment of a family day on Saturdays, then figure out what is making you the most tired, make some changes, and measure if it's working by your Saturday energy.

NOTIFY: Do you know someone who is very good at saying no or seems to be managing their time well? Is there someone you admire who you could ask to help you figure some things out?

Sometimes it can look like other people have an advantage over you. Maybe they are better liked or have a college degree that you don't or they just seem lucky. Don't be fooled by this temptation to assume you are at an unchangeable disadvantage. These people have worked hard at what they have (degrees don't come easy!), and they may have insight for you. If you admire them, then it is probably at least partly because they are kind and generous. I doubt you'd be admiring the company jerk who tattles his way to the top. Ask them to lunch or if you could have a phone call sometime. Write your questions down and pray beforehand.

Leave your excuses at the door. You don't have to do what they recommend, but when you're interacting with them, just listen and have an open mind. If you keep telling them reasons why you can't do what they suggest, then you're wasting their time.

CHANGE: Set aside time each year to evaluate your outside-the-home activities and timetables. Because you generally make a commitment, you usually can't just quit anytime. But you can make plans to move on or leave when the time is right if that's what you decide.

Or an activity may be the right thing to be doing but needs some altering. Maybe your hours could shift or your responsibilities need to change. Do the people you work with know what your limits are? Do you need to talk with them so you're not constantly frustrated?

Once you have evaluated your time, what is working, and some changes you want to make, it's important to stick to your plan. People will always ask you for more—more time, more help, more commitments until you are right back where you started. They don't know your needs for your life and family any more than you know theirs. If you feel that you are being generous with your decisions, then that's enough. Be strong, sister!

This quote from *The Best Yes* says it beautifully: "At the end of the day, a healthy relationship isn't void of service. Of course we must serve, love, give, be available, help, and contribute to the greater good. But we must have the freedom to say yes or no responsibly without fear of emotional consequences."[5]

Endure: Ahhh, enduring, the most important part of all. This isn't the hardest place to find balance, but it can get touchy since people won't like your refusals. It can even cost you some relationships. But those aren't valuable relationships if they can't withstand you changing your commitments.

Be nice, help those who are depending on you through whatever transition you are making, and then be at peace about it.

I know I talk a lot here about quitting or leaving an area of work. That's because most people are far too overcommitted. But that's not the only change you might make. You could just need to reduce some hours or shift some of your work to someone else. It could be that you need to do *more* community or church ministry instead of devoting time to a paying job. I have certainly hit points where I realized that I was not doing anything for anyone outside of my family.

You know what? That's okay when you're in the middle of raising babies and young children. Your whole existence right now is meant to raise them, and it's fine as long as you're still praying and getting out once in a while. (If I didn't get out occasionally, you'd have to put me in a straitjacket and take me away to the loony hospital.) But if you are in a place where you can reach out of your home, find ways to do that. If you don't have a car, do work online. If you think you don't have any skills, work at Chick-fil-A, volunteer at the nursing home, mow your neighbor's yard, help at a food pantry, take a course on being a virtual assistant; the possibilities are endless.

Serving others is an important part of our well-being. We need to know that we are doing something good for others, even if it's the simple gesture of handing them their ticket through the window at the movie theater. Paid or not, the reward is in helping someone else. Find a way to use the talents that God gave you to do something for someone else!

ASSIGNMENT

As you look through your activities both outside of home and within, find an hour each week that you can keep free. Then during that time, every week, read the Bible and pray. If you're lost about how to begin, ask a friend or go to a local Christian bookstore and ask for a book that will help you. Keep notes of what you're praying about, and use the time to really focus on Jesus.

THE BLESSING OF FRIENDS

For if they fall, one will lift up his fellow. But woe to him who is alone when he falls and has not another to lift him up!

Ecclesiastes 4:10

FRIENDSHIPS THAT LAST

This is one of my favorite events in my life. I can only assume it is because I laughed harder than I ever had before or since.

My good friend Sharra and I decided to travel for a weekend to a huge flea market in east Texas. We packed our bags (she took a bag entirely for shoes, although I have never understood why), emptied all the bench seats from my fifteen-passenger van, loaded up, and took off. We blasted music on the six-hour drive, strategized routes for the flea market, made a food list, and braced ourselves for a fantastic weekend.

The whole time together at the flea market was a mix of highs and lows. One minute we'd find a great deal on a treasure and the next our van would get stuck in the mud or we would lose our money. It seemed like each mix-up got worse and worse until we found ourselves on the side of the road in a van that wouldn't start. In the middle of a small Texas town six hours from home. With a dead cell-phone battery.

But Sharra is the kind of friend who brings out the best in any situation. Instead of getting more and more upset, we started to laugh harder and harder at each new obstacle. A stranger fixed our van at midnight in the local Walmart parking lot. We had to push it into a position where the front was facing a streetlight, which made it hard for drivers going by to tell that the mechanic was standing there with his head under the open hood. In other words, we looked to any passerby like we were two gals standing next to a huge industrial van with its hood open, stranded. Creepy men kept slowing down to offer us rides, and each time the nice mechanic who gave up a date night with his wife to help us would pop up from behind the van and tell them to go away.

On the way home we decided that after a long weekend like that we deserved to treat ourselves to a stop at IKEA. For me, there is nothing more soothing than an hour inside the mothership to help me relax. The stop was about three hours from the flea market hotel where we had spent the weekend, and about two hours into the drive I told Sharra that I needed to use the bathroom. It was a long stretch of empty highway, and by the time we found a suitable restroom, we were only ten minutes from IKEA, so I decided to wait until we got there.

Along the last few minutes of the drive we started to reflect on our crazy weekend until we got to laughing really hard. It was just such a ridiculous string of events! And Sharra always makes me laugh harder; she's just that kind of friend.

I finally pulled into the IKEA parking lot and told her, "I am going to have to run to the bathroom. I have to go *bad*!" She told me to run and she'd catch up. That was my plan, but just as my feet hit the ground (it's a big drop out of the fifteen-passenger van to the ground), she said something that struck me as really, really funny. To this day neither of us can remember what she said because what happened next was too dramatic and has blocked out her comment.

I slammed the door of the big van and got about three steps toward the store when my laughing turned into full-on hilarious guffawing and I lost all control. Of my bladder. Right then and there in the IKEA parking lot I started to pee. Not just a little either, a lot. Sharra, wondering why I hadn't come around from my side of the van yet, stepped around to check on me and found me standing still, laughing as hard as I could and dripping from beneath my skirt. The look of sheer horror on her face made me laugh more as she shouted, "Make it stop! What is wrong with you? *Stop peeing!*" But I couldn't. The laughing had completely taken over all of my faculties. Once I stopped, I told her I had gotten my shoes totally wet and I would need to change them. But I only had one pair with me, so I asked to borrow one from her shoe suitcase. "No way!" she told me firmly. "You're not going to wet on any of *my* shoes!" That only made me laugh harder.

I wore her down, and eventually she pulled out her least favorite pair and told me to keep them.

I put on the shoes, got cleaned up with some rinsing and using the bathroom hand dryer, and we continued our plans to shop around in IKEA. I know that the laughing and the mess would have stopped some people, but it's IKEA; I had no choice.

That weekend will go down in my memory as one of the best times I've ever had. The broken-down van and the puddle in the IKEA parking lot are gone now, but the memories of laughing so hard that I was sore for three days afterward live on.

FYI: I realize that I have told you two pee stories and you may feel concerned for my bladder health. Don't worry. I may have a slightly higher tendency to lose control after having so many babies, but it really happens very rarely. But when it does, it's so funny that I have to share the experience.

THE BEST KINDS OF FRIENDS

My friends are what hold me together most of the time. I have a small circle of very close women friends who I know would do anything for me, and the commitment is mutual. I don't worry about them betraying me or judging me or gossiping about me. But it took a long, long time and a lot of water under these bridges for me to know I could trust these women that much.

We go out for dinner a few times a month and it is always, always a blessing! We talk about our kids and how we are dealing with hard issues and things we've seen on social media. Then all of a sudden, out of the blue, one of us will say something that sends the whole group into fits of laughter. That starts a domino effect of silliness that generally gets loud enough to disturb the table next to us. Then we get serious again as one of us shares a deep hurt or trial, and we all pray together and offer thoughts or advice. We finish and head home long after the restaurant kicks us out. Our time together is like the spinning of the carousel, around and around until we have worn ourselves out from the joy of it all.

God gives us our friends to grow us, comfort us, encourage us, challenge us, support us, need us, serve us, admonish us, build us, bless us, and mostly bear each other's burdens (Gal. 6:2). God made us to crave time with friends and have relationships. He wants us to depend on each other and truly know each other. If you don't have these kinds of friends in your life, I encourage you to ask God for them. Pray, and also keep your mind open. The person He wants to bring into your life may be someone you least expect.

What we have to guard ourselves from is replacing God with our friends. They are not our identity, our source of strength, or our salvation. Friends can lift you to the throne of grace through prayer and encouragement, but they can't impart the grace to you. Only God can do that. When a friend becomes the first thing you think of in the day, the one you want to talk to before you talk to God, who you look to for your affirmation, you have made the friend an idol.

I love anything by C. S. Lewis, and this quote from his book *The Four Loves* puts it so beautifully: "We may give our human lives the unconditional allegiance which we owe only to God. Then they become gods: then they become demons. Then they will destroy us, and also destroy themselves. For natural loves that are allowed to become gods do not remain loves. They are still called so, but can become in fact complicated forms of hatred."[1]

GETTING OUT OF BALANCE

Friendships can get out of balance in our lives very easily. There are many, many ways this can happen. Sometimes you are the one who is causing the imbalance; often it is the other person, but mostly it is both of you not pointing each other to Christ that causes the breakdown.

I have been in all of these positions. I have been too needy, too selfish, or too naive. As I got older, I found myself occasionally on the receiving end of a selfish person who was unable to accept my boundaries. But most of my torn or damaged relationships have been because both of us lost our sight of how to keep a friendship healthy and safe.

Unlike family relationships, we get to choose these people. Oh, wait, or do we? Sometimes God does the choosing. Did Jonathan and David choose each other? The Bible says that God knit the soul of Jonathan with the soul of David. Them's some strong ties! But because God did the knitting, we can be sure it was for their best. In my lifetime there have been a few friends whom I know God knit me together with. It's undeniable when you just understand each other and are dedicated to each other's well-being. These are very rare, however, and you have only a few in a lifetime. Those friendships of mine I nurture very carefully because I know their value in my life.

But most friends pass through, or in and out, over the years. Isn't it funny how our kids are convinced that their junior high friends will be their lifelong buddies? I just smile and nod and refrain from telling them that very few people even know where those friends live after five years.

Often a friendship can just kind of drift away—no reason, no pain involved. That's not the kind of friends we are discussing in this chapter. Those don't really get out of balance because they aren't vital in your life. You aren't going to fight for them, and when they've moved on, you hardly notice, even if you really liked them. That is normal and natural. We can't remain friends with everyone we have met or interacted with in life.

THREE KINDS OF FRIENDS

There are, in my experience, three main friend categories. First, the BFF, the best friend forever. This is a genuine, "lasts for years (or life)," "there for each other through thick and thin" kind of friend. Second is the GF, the good friend. She is reliable and you really like her, hang out with her, and occasionally do things for each other, but you know she won't ever be in the innermost circle (this could be for many reasons). Last is the AF, the affiliate friend. This is someone you connect with through an outside source. She can be a neighbor who you see on the street occasionally, the woman you talk to sometimes at church, another mom at your child's school, a Facebook friend, and so on. You don't count on these people for anything, but you're connected in some way and they're usually nice enough. You might chat with them sometimes or invite them to a party.

Sometimes people will move back and forth between the second and third categories. But rarely will anyone who drifts out of the first get back on that list. The BFF column is the most carefully guarded. It can happen, but not usually. And of course, there are levels within levels of each category because, well, women are complicated. We are like many-layered onions, only we smell better.

Knowing which category your friends are in helps when you are making purposeful choices about how or when to find balance in these relationships. More time and effort would go into a category-one friendship, of course, than a three. But please hear me when I say that we love them all! There are no levels in God's sight, and this is just our human way of making life work. Everyone ultimately has the same value to God and therefore to us. It's just that we can't pour ourselves into everyone and we have room for only a few BFFs in our lives. He won't knit your heart together with many people; in His wisdom He knows that wouldn't be good for us.

In the book *Balancing It All*, Candace Cameron Bure said this about friendships: "As you think about what it looks like to maintain balance in your life, I want to encourage you to evaluate your friendships. Do you have at least one good friend who you can trust? Do you have friends who share your faith and values? Do you also have friends who help you to understand and respect other viewpoints?"[2]

I love that last sentence because life is so much richer if we have friends who are different from us! Having people in our lives from other ethnicities, lifestyles, political views, etc. adds so much color to our little spot on the planet. I don't have to agree with you to call you my friend. These categories can help if you're struggling to find friends who have different beliefs than you. You don't have to put everyone in the BFF category. If you're stuck in a rut with your friends, ask God to send you someone who will challenge you in new ways and open your world up a little!

BREAKING DOWN

Even the best friendships break down occasionally. Anything from disagreements to moving hundreds of miles away can dissolve a treasured relationship. Geography, while not absolutely essential, matters when it comes to friends.

I have many friends in the GF category who live all over the country; some even around the world! I love them all dearly and try to stay connected, but not being able to help when a child is sick or sit down together in person is an inhibitor when it comes to close friendships. My two BFFs both live in my town and they know when I need help because they can see my gray roots or that I have gained weight. Once when I picked up one of them to meet the other ladies for dinner, she got in my car and said, "Uh-oh, your car is messy. Something's wrong. What can I do to help?" She knows me well enough to understand what is normal for me, and I am a clean-car freak. You can't get that from a distance relationship.

So what happens when a friendship, of any category, gets out of whack? This happens so often that I know with certainty that it's happened to you. No one gets away with a life without friend battles; it just isn't possible. And I would go so far as to say that you have been a problem to other friends from time to time. And you know what? It's okay! We learn, we repent, we do our best, and we move on, sometimes without that person in our lives.

God says in Romans 12:18, "If possible, so far as it depends on you, live peaceably with all." Don't miss that part about what depends on you. You can't control other people, and as long as you know that you have left your bitterness and self-righteousness behind, then you are okay. That doesn't mean you will automatically have peaceful relationships. You can only do what you can do. If you have apologized when you did something wrong and you genuinely mean it and are trying to make a change in the area where you made a mistake, then that's all you can do. If your friend doesn't accept that, then that is her issue. You have done what depends on you.

Let's talk about what can get out of balance in a friendship. Women are such multilayered (okay, I will just say it, kinda crazy) creatures that when you put two or more of us together it can get risky. Even the best of friends can be like two cats in the same cage, fighting for the best ball of catnip. So often a teeny tiny miscommunication turns into a bigger issue until it becomes like a cancer to the relationship. It seems so small at first; she says something hurtful or selfish and you react badly. You both decide to brush it off, but it doesn't really go away. Ever so slowly you are seeing your conversations through the lens of bitterness, and eventually, it falls apart. You both feel wronged, you both think it's ultimately the other person's fault, and in the end the friendship falls apart.

One book I love on this topic of being hurt is *Wounded by God's People* by Anne Graham Lotz. She was bitterly hurt by her church friends and shared this: "If the person who has wounded you, or has been wounded by you, rejects your forgiving words or gestures and refuses to move towards reconciliation, take it to Jesus in prayer. He understands what it feels like to make every effort to reconcile, only to be rejected. The relationship may never be reconciled, but Jesus can heal you—and your memories."[3]

So how do we stop this from happening? As I said before, we can be responsible only for our part in the problem, which can be enough to turn the sinking ship around and steer it back to safety.

THE BALANCE

BEGIN: Don't put it off; as soon as you detect a problem, you need to face it and deal with it. If you are not going to deal with it immediately with your friend, then deal with it immediately in your heart.

ASSESS: If you know where the problem started, then you are already halfway there. It is often pretty easy to determine the source of the break. A small argument, a late arrival to an important event, a forgotten appointment, a rude remark—something that might normally be insignificant but this time it didn't die for some reason. Step back and unpack the moment of the crack in the friendship. Did you overreact? Had you been kind of feeling hurt over similar instances in the past and were holding it in? Is this an issue that you could have been more honest about? Did you contribute to the mess in any way? Are you also reacting out of previous hurt that wasn't caused by your friend? Try to look at the problem objectively and see if maybe you need to let go of some of the blame and forgive your friend. I recommend asking your husband. Mine is great at seeing things in me that I miss because I am too close.

LEARN: There is *no* shortage of wisdom in this area in God's Word! He knew we would struggle with relationships, so He gave us a heap of help. In every letter from Paul to the various churches, he dispensed wisdom for how to treat one another. Jesus said to the disciples in John 13:34, "A new commandment I give to you, that you love one another: just as I have loved you, you also are to love one another." I notice He left out the part about me having to love only the people who are nice to me. Drats! That would have been so much easier!

There are many, many examples in Scripture about how to treat each other, so I will leave it to you to look up some for yourself. But one of my favorites is when Paul told the Romans in verse 14:13, "Therefore let us not pass judgment on one another any longer, but rather decide never to put a stumbling block or hindrance in the way of a brother." He was not referring to holding each other accountable to sin, but rather that we should place our focus on how we affect one another instead of being so critical. Pay more attention to your own influence on your friends and less on their behavior.

ACCOUNT: How can you measure a friendship problem? Well, the first thing I want to impress is that you can *not* use feelings to measure anything. Emotions are unpredictable, unstable, and no way to determine how something is working. Here are a few ideas for measuring friendship struggles: Look for something special in your unique relationship, and watch for that to grow or decline. If you used to share your victories with each other, note if that has changed. Or maybe you have been noticing her flaws more than you used to. See that for what it is—a change in the relationship that you can evaluate. You could also measure the amount of repair needed by the way she seems to hold back.

In the case of a BFF, you definitely want to prayerfully get any problem out in the open and discuss it. I don't mean tell her every little offense, but if it's something you're really struggling with, be honest. Holding in a hurt can turn ugly fast. If it's a GF, you need to be discerning about how far to go with the efforts to repair. Sometimes we are wise to simply pray for her, show an extra measure of grace and kindness, and be available to talk, but not push it. But for an AF, I think it's generally best to just let things go. No one is perfect or will meet your every expectation, and if it's not a relationship that you are investing much in, then trying to point out hurts and disappointments will usually only do further damage.

If you haven't read *Beyond Boundaries* by Dr. John Townsend, then it needs to go on your must-read list. It gives some great relationship measuring tools: "Aside from looking at hurt and harm, ask yourself, 'Is the relationship worth the time and energy I put into it?' Some relationships are and some are not. You only have so much time and energy. You need to steward your time well just as you need to steward your finances well. When you buy stocks or invest in a business, you expect a return on your investment. The same is true in relationships; something good should happen— increased love, connection, intimacy, building a life together."[4]

NOTIFY: Figuring out how to proceed with a friendship problem is not an easy decision, and it's best to get input. Be discreet, and seek wise advice without gossiping or exposing someone else's flaws.

CHANGE: Now move ahead carefully. Friendships are as fragile as a flower, and just as beautiful! Once you've found a piece of the relationship that you can give some TLC to, don't jump in and start banging things around. It's when we speak out quickly that we make matters worse. A favorite verse of mine that helps me when I am ready to confront a problem with a friend is James 1:19: "Know this, my beloved brothers: let every person be quick to hear, slow to speak, slow to anger." Oh boy has that wisdom come in handy many times! If you are struggling with how to move forward, try listening! Then proceed with caution and with your Bible knowledge at the ready (to keep you from acting poorly, not to prove you are right about something), and step out in love.

ENDURE: Whatever happens, sometimes it takes awhile to repair a damaged friendship. Be patient with yourself as you make mistakes and don't always act "perfectly." Be patient with your friend as she figures out how to recover from her own hurt.

Remember, everyone is hurt when a friendship gets out of balance. Your hurt doesn't trump her hurt and vice versa. Being loving and patient with her, even when it gets difficult, may be what brings the relationship back into a good balance.

These principles work for any kind of unbalanced friendship whether it is with your child's schoolteacher whom you like but just can't agree with on some things or it is with a dear friend whom you trust to lay down her life for you. Most of the time, with a mature attitude and some understanding of the healthy steps it takes to right an off-kilter relationship, we can steer the ship back into safe waters.

But occasionally, sadly, a friendship won't be repaired. Nevertheless, you can still take steps to find balance, even if it's just for yourself.

THE COMPLETELY BROKEN FRIENDSHIP

I have had relationships break down, and sometimes, no matter what I tried, the other person would not let go of her disappointment in me. As painful as that is to go through, I have developed a bit of a thick skin when it comes to being rejected. It would have seemed impossible to me a few years ago that I could have survived some of the pain that has come my way through broken friendships. But I tell you, I have learned some beautiful lessons from those lost relationships, and I am so much stronger than I could have ever been without enduring those experiences. I mean, I am not going to be writing any of those lost friends a thank-you note, but I am incredibly grateful for what God did for me through those trials.

A broken friendship can be one of the most painful experiences. I have been through some extremely difficult betrayals, and I know how much you hurt. Many women are suffering the same quiet grief. There is a comforter who wants to relieve you of your pain through His mercy and grace. He is the best friend you will ever have and the only One who will never, ever reject you no matter what you do. He knows firsthand how much it hurts to be betrayed by someone you trust.

If you are recovering from a painful broken friendship, let me offer some comfort by saying that you are not alone in your suffering. Christ Himself was betrayed by His closest friends. Judas, I mean, wow. That had to feel like a kick in the gut to Jesus even if He did know it was coming. But also Peter, who denied Christ three times, turned out to be a less-than-stellar friend. And in the amazing way Christ does, He forgave them. It doesn't seem possible sometimes to forgive, especially those who hurt us on purpose. But Christ is there to stand with you and be your comforter and peace giver. He knows exactly how you feel!

TAKING CARE OF YOURSELF

Although you won't restore all relationships, you can restore your faith in other people, release your pain, and have complete hope and joy again. It is a long process, but God will take you through it. He promises to do that for you.

When it's time to let go of a friendship, you must turn your focus of balance onto yourself. Take a long look at whether you gave too much of your heart to that person and not enough to your relationship with God. In Proverbs 23:26, God said, "My son, give me your heart, and let your eyes observe my ways." He wants our hearts! And we are to look to Him for how to act and respond, not to our friends and not to people's opinions of us. Just because that neighbor refuses to like you doesn't mean you are doing anything wrong.

Looking to God for your answers is the *best* way to protect your heart. Give it to Him, hear what He tells you through the Holy Spirit, and trust Him to take care of what you cannot control. Yes, live peaceably, but don't sacrifice your heart to do it! And when it comes to the heart, if you are giving it to Him, then you will have an easier time loving those difficult people despite how hard it feels.

C. S. Lewis said in *Mere Christianity*, "The rule for us all is perfectly simple. Do not waste time bothering whether you love your neighbor; act as if you did. As soon as we do this we find one of the great secrets. When you are behaving as if you loved someone, you will presently come to love him."[5]

Keep your focus on God, ask Him to help you show love to those who don't deserve it, remember who you are in Christ, and walk on.

ASSIGNMENT

I am a list girl, mostly because my mind doesn't work effectively on its own. I make lists for everything. I have a cute notebook (because it needs to be cute, of course) that I carry around with me and just keep lists in it. So to wrap up our discussion about friends, let's make a list.

Write down all of your friends' names. Then give each a code of BFF, GF, or AF (but keep that list to yourself or you could hurt people!). Next, preferably in another color pen because everything is better in multicolor, write beside each code what you think you are to the person, either BFF, GF, or AF. You may be surprised to discover that several of your relationships are not the same for you as they are to your friends. Evaluating that can help you keep a balance in these relationships. If my neighbor is an AF to me but I know that I am probably a GF to her, I treat her with the respect that she has given me by inviting me into that circle.

Once you've got your list and codes, next to the names jot down a few ideas of ways you can improve or balance these relationships. Even though, if you're like me, you won't actually *do* everything on your list (because who has time for that?), it will make you more aware of what each person needs and how you can work with that knowledge.

And lastly, enjoy your friends! Girlfriends are a gift from God like no other. They will bring you chocolate, let you talk for hours, and if it's a mature, wise friend, she will feed you God's Word. Love them. Bless them. Be thankful for them!

9

MONEY MATTERS

*Keep your life free from love of money, and be content with what
you have, for he has said, "I will never leave you nor forsake you."*

Hebrews 13:5

THE SONIC TEST

My husband, James, is a receipt-a-holic. He wants the receipt for
everything, and I am what is known in medical terms as "receipt
challenged." If my child's life depended on me locating a receipt, I
still don't think I could do it. I puh-romise you I do try! I keep special envelopes in my purse, and once I bought this nice wallet that
held receipts really well. I even have a designated receipt drawer
where I'm supposed to put them when I get home from shopping
and James can retrieve them. If there is a receipt system out there,
I have tried it. It's like dieting, only meaner.

So one weekend James and I were planning to have our first
official weekend alone since having kids. Our oldest two were old
enough for us to leave for one night, so we decided to go together
to a homeschool convention that was a few hours away. Yep, we
know how to have a good time.

I spent the week beforehand prepping food for the kids and
making sure we had neighbors in place whom they could call in
an emergency. I was so excited to be footloose and fancy-free with

my husband. As we said our final good-byes to the kids and got in the car and closed the doors, I was practically giddy. "Here we go!" I said, delighted.

James looked over at me and said, "Okay, there is something I need to talk to you about first thing, before we even leave the driveway."

I felt the happy juice drain out of my system. *Oh great, what is he going to say that will kill my good time?*

He continued, "Lisa, I know you will be spending money this weekend and buying school curriculum for the kids, and that's fine; we made our budget for that, and I know you'll stick to it. But what I really need you to do is keep *every single* receipt. So I made you this envelope [picture him reaching across from the driver's side, in front of my knees, opening the glove compartment and pulling out a normal legal-sized paper envelope with the words 'Lisa's Receipts' written across the front in pencil] to keep your receipts in from this weekend."

Somehow, and I really still don't get this even years later, he thought this would strike me as a romantic gesture.

I was insulted and deflated. All I wanted was two relaxing days alone with my husband, and before we even pulled out of the driveway, it had gone terribly wrong. I held the envelope, pouting as he started down the road. I was quietly thinking of how to respond to this childlike treatment.

Finally, he asked me what was wrong and I let it all out like opening a fire hydrant. (For the full effect, you have to read this in a very whiny, mostly crying voice.) "I am a grown woman and I try so hard to keep the receipts for you and all I wanted was to have a good time together and you know how hard I try and I can't believe you made me this stupid envelope like I am a two-year-old," and on and on it went.

So maybe I tend to be dramatic; whatever, I was hurt. I put the envelope in my purse and agreed to keep *every* receipt, and we agreed to just stop talking about it.

We drove on in silence for about an hour when I asked him to stop at Sonic so I could get a cup of ice (just one of my many obsessions). He pulled in, and while I waited for the carhop to deliver my order, James got out and went to the restroom.

When he got back in, I was starting to relax and we talked for a few minutes when he asked me, "Did you put the Sonic receipt in your envelope?"

"No," I said, "they don't give you receipts at Sonic."

"Yes, they do," he informed me just as confidently. "They put it on your cup with a sticker."

"No," I said, digging around in the trash bag to prove my point. "All they stick to your cup is a coupon and I threw it away."

I pulled the wadded-up sticker paper out of the trash and handed it to him. He proceeded to try to unstick the mess until he finally had it flat, then held it right up to my face. "What is *this*?"

Oh. It's a receipt.

The shame.

Okay, okay, so maybe I did need a special elementary school child envelope. I could kind of see his point.

I took the Sonic receipt and, with a pen from my purse, drew a huge smiley face on it and stuck it to the rearview mirror. "This," I announced, "is the symbol of my apology and my promise to keep every receipt from the whole weekend."

He grinned and accepted my apology.

And that receipt stayed stuck to my rearview mirror for a whole year. Why? Because sometimes I need a little reminder of how much I have to learn and how often I mess up and how even the hardest lesson can be made better with a giant smiley face.

DOLLARS AND CENTS

Managing money is one of those earthly things that we have to do to survive, but while how we handle money is important, wealth is not important to God. He wants us to love Him more than money. But I still have to pay my bills, right? It takes up a lot of our time and effort to reconcile bank accounts, make budgets, and figure out how to afford unexpected expenses. Some people even have too much money, and believe it or not, that creates all kinds of difficulties from people begging for handouts to knowing where to keep it safely and not pay it all to the government.

In the first twenty years of our marriage, we scraped by and at least twice a month it was a bit like desperation—we were barely hanging on. I can remember going to the grocery store with fewer than fifty dollars in cash and trying to figure out how to feed my large family for the week. No treats, no extras. It was bare bones for many years. I'd walk around the store with a list and write down the exact price of each item I set in the shopping cart. Then at the end I would find an unoccupied aisle, hide there, and add up the numbers. If it totaled more than fifty, I would dig through the cart, remove what we could live without, and put it back on the shelf. I would see women with overfilled carts, carelessly adding bags of chips and cartons of soda to their piles and wonder if I would ever be able to do that.

The good news is that there are many things you can do about financial problems. Escaping them is a climb and it takes time, but it is possible for you to move out of a place of squeezing every penny. With strength and perseverance I did make it out of the "fifty dollars per week for eleven people" place.

Finances are a booger. I know it's a gross word, but let's see money for what it really is. First, it's green—duh. Second, it causes headaches and chaos and takes up way more energy than it should. Third, it's a small thing that takes up more of your energy than it should. And fourth, it's just a *pain*.

I have to tell you that I am married to a CPA and tax attorney. He is a numbers guy who wants every receipt and an accounting of what I spend down to the penny. He checks our accounts every day, and he thinks spreadsheets are romantic. So I just may have an overly exaggerated distaste for dealing with money issues.

But even the normal person who doesn't read tax magazines for fun (did you even know there were tax magazines?) has a love-hate relationship with money. Sure, it's nice when you can pay for the things you need and have a little extra in the bank for a rainy day. But you have to spend gobs of time adding it up, balancing the accounts, planning ahead, doing taxes, figuring out insurance, paying bills—*blech*! (Before you think my hubs is a financial control freak, let me tell you I adore how cautious he is and I am unbelievably grateful for his guidance and leadership!)

Money can take a perfectly pleasant day and turn it into a nightmare in an instant. Just trying to agree with your spouse on how to use what little extra you have, or which bills to pay first, or what to do when the tires need replacing can cause one to go into a depression.

I'M IN LOVE WITH DAVE RAMSEY

As you can imagine, my husband has a bit of a man crush on Dave. I mean, what Christian CPA doesn't love a guy who teaches people how to take better care of their money and get out of debt?!

But because I am also part of the relationship (for you Dave Ramsey fans, guess which one of us is the "free spirit"), our financial partnership has never been smooth sailing. I know God wanted to challenge our marriage through our finances.

One thing that's so great about Dave is that he helps to bring a husband and wife together over issues of finances. He understands the free spirit in me, and he embraces the nerd in my husband. He is the one who told James that I need a little "Lisa" money. And that concept has lifted a huge burden off me. I mean, my constant whining was even starting to wear me down.

At first it was about twenty dollars a month in the "Lisa" account. There wasn't much I could do with twenty dollars, but the freedom of being able to spend it on anything I wanted without reporting where it went was lovely. I loved my sweet husband for his willingness to conform to this.

What I discovered was that if I would scrimp and not spend it for a month, I would actually have forty dollars to spend. That got me all excited, and I saved more. Eventually I developed some mad skills and have bought furniture, taken road trips, and even remodeled the kitchen with my "Lisa" money. It was a little like the loaves and fishes story; when I was ready to listen to what Jesus was trying to tell me, He multiplied the reward in miraculous ways.

Here's something Dave's book *The Legacy Journey* has to say about enjoying your money: "According to Solomon, the wisest man who ever lived, part of managing our God-given wealth is honoring God with our enjoyment of that blessing."[1]

THE CURSE OF DEBT

Here in the good old US of A, we have bought into the lie that it's perfectly fine to borrow money. I am not an expert, but even I can see that buying a computer with credit at 18 percent can make an $800 computer actually cost you more than $1,500! You paid *way* too much for that device, my friend!

But we want it now and we need the latest thing. Clothing manufacturers convince us that plaid is a must-have for the season, car companies show ads with celebrities that cause us to drool over the newest technology, even cereal boxes draw us in and take over our brains. *Buy me! You need me! Who cares what I cost? You're getting sleeepeee …*

My wonderful friends, this is not me standing at the top of a mountain looking down on your money mistakes and crying,

"Look out, dummy!" This is me standing right there with you, barely out of the shackles of debt and financial ruin. I know of what I speak.

Personally, I am crazy about remodeling, and when I get it in my head that a room needs changing, a charging bull would be easier to stop. I am like the girl in *Willy Wonka* who wanted her golden goose and didn't care who she had to step on to get it. Sure, I will make a budget and try to be as frugal as possible, but occasionally I step ahead of the cash flow. Everyone has a weak area of spending (personally I have five or six), and we have to train ourselves to be grateful for what we have and not spend beyond our limits.

I wonder what would happen if we all decided to start living the lives God gives us instead of forcing a lifestyle that we want. Can you imagine how many car dealerships and Best Buys would go under? Now, I don't want to put anyone out of business. I just want to show you that there is a better way! I still buy computers and cars; I just pay for them now with cash that I have.

Here's the thing: there is a level of pain that is naturally imparted when you spend your hard-earned money on something. If I save for a year to buy a new couch, search for the perfect one, and pay for it out of pocket, it's a little painful to watch that money go out of my account. It's been nice sitting on that cushion for a year and I have a measure of pride that I was able to save that. But now it's gone. Sure, I have a gorgeous sofa in its place, but we are supposed to feel that hurt. It's what keeps us in balance.

When we go ahead and buy the couch on credit, don't wait and don't save, we never actually see that pile of money in our account and we don't have that pride of accomplishment. What happens is that credit-card purchase actually robs us of our natural need for the agony of letting go of the money and we don't fully learn from the sacrifice. There is no pain, no sacrifice; it's just fifty dollars a month and no big deal. We are tricked into thinking it doesn't matter, but ultimately we lose the true joy that comes from building our lives slowly and in God's timing.

FREEDOM!

I wish it were possible for me to pour out to you the freedom I now live with. It took years, I mean *years*, for us to dig ourselves out of a hole of debt and depression. We chipped away at it, dug ourselves deeper sometimes, made new budgets and fresh plans, generated extra income, and did everything we could to pay off the credit-card debt that we had accumulated. I know the weighty burden of debt. When God says in Proverbs 22:7, "The borrower is the slave of the lender," He's not kidding! I was a slave and in bondage by my own choices.

In the end, I had to stop my spending and we had to dig ourselves out over time. It was a long time, but I am happy to say we finally broke through the ginormous wall we had built around our finances and it is lovely on the other side. But don't get the idea that it was a huge one-swing crash. No, that wall came down one brick at a time and it left us with calluses and injury.

In *The Legacy Journey*, Dave Ramsey wrote, "The best way to eat an elephant is one bite at a time, and the best way to move towards your life's calling is one steady step at a time. So focus on finding work that matters, and then shift into living out your dream with passion and purpose. This is called your Road to Awesome."[2]

Do I wish we had never gotten into debt in the first place? Yes. But the lessons we learned were so hard and so complete that I believe the experience will save us from worse mistakes in the future. No matter where you are in your financial journey, there is hope. Read Dave's books, borrow them from the library, and don't get discouraged. You are one of the millions of people struggling with this.

THE UNSEEN STRUGGLE

When you struggle with weight or broken friendships or a messy house, everyone can see that. But when broken finances are your burden, it's easily covered up—at least for a time. Your neighbor's new car or the vacation your husband's boss took with his family look so appealing and we can quickly begin to envy their situation. But don't always believe what you see. People don't present themselves for what they truly are anymore. I would venture to say that most of those people are not what they seem. They may even be in financial trouble.

Money and possessions are no way to measure happiness or success. True joy in life is living an honest, peaceful life with your family and friends. Spending your life trying to impress others with what you can buy is an empty life and leads to destruction.

Let go of the jealousy and envy over someone else's nice home and gorgeous jewelry. Those things mean nothing! Who are the people on the inside, behind the walls? You may never know who is struggling and unhappy. You might spot a woman at the mall who has great taste and the money to back it up. But believe you me she deals with problems with money and her life is not a bed of roses. Even if she isn't dealing with debt, she might have trouble keeping up with her checkbook or fight with her husband over spending, or she might struggle with deadbeat family members always expecting her to give them some of her cash. My friend, money is at the heart of many problems, and no one is immune to them.

SO TELL ME, HOW ARE YOU?

Well? Are you struggling with money in some way? The most common problem is debt with not enough coming in to keep up with it. When you're young, you naturally struggle. Your career hasn't taken off yet, and rent isn't cheap. You need transportation and a phone and that silly stuff called food. It's rough. We've all been there. Then in your thirties when you think it should be getting easier, it doesn't because you now have a few kids and a mortgage to think about.

What is your issue in managing money? I promise, this is actually one of the easiest of the nine areas to handle because for the most part you are battling only yourself. The victory is in your hands. Even though you have a husband as a partner and maybe he is the free spirit, you can come to a place of agreement and work together. This doesn't involve other people. I know how it feels when the collections agency calls and rudely threatens you, but the decisions are yours. You have the power to turn this around!

BALANCE

BEGIN: Oddly, while this is one area that we have the most control over, it can be the hardest to begin. We don't like to make sacrifices. But it's time.

ASSESS: Look at your financial situation from a distance. What would you see if you were not directly involved? Would you see disorganization or unnecessary spending? It's so much easier to look at other people's problems without all the emotional baggage tied to them and to locate the problem.

Keep your goals in mind when assessing the problem. Do you want to get out of debt or just be able to pay your bills more easily? Do you want to save money to buy a house or take a family vacation? Or do you just want to be able to buy groceries without worry? You may have multilayered goals and need to assess each level individually, then build a plan. When we were in our darkest time financially, our immediate goal may have been just to get the creditors off our backs and then work our way up.

But don't let the more obvious problems mask the deeper issues. When you assess, look at where you spend the most money and what you pay for that you don't really need. What emotional burden are you trying to lift through spending? I personally like a little bit of shopping therapy, but when it becomes a burden on my family either though overspending or filling the house with junk, I have to take a look at my own heart.

Even my buddy Dave says the amount needed is different for everyone. You have to look at your own set of circumstances and not at your neighbor's.

LEARN: Even though there will be no need for money in heaven, God addressed it. His Word has wisdom about treasures and idols and loving money more than God that we can heed. When you are struggling with your finances, the Bible is where you will find comfort. It will guide and direct you not only in how to let go of the love for money but also in how to find peace for your burden:

> Do not lay up for yourselves treasures on earth, where moth and rust destroy and where thieves break in and steal, but lay up for yourselves treasures in heaven, where neither moth nor rust destroys and where thieves do not break in and steal. For where your treasure is, there your heart will be also. (Matt. 6:19–21)

ACCOUNT: Money itself is a form of measurement. Cents, dollars, hundreds, negative hundreds. Yep, been there. It takes a brave soul to spread it all out, have every penny accounted for and all the bills represented, and really look at the whole picture, but it is so worth knowing where you stand! Sure, the outcome of the information gathering may be depression and a temptation to be hopeless, but at least you know the basic math. Sometimes that old southern adage "You can't squeeze blood from a turnip" applies. But there is hope.

NOTIFY: I am not talking about asking for money or borrowing money (I think we have thoroughly covered that nightmare). I mean asking for advice and holding yourself accountable. If you have looked at the whole picture and made an action plan, even if it is short term, you want someone to hold you accountable. Old habits die hard; we find our identities in what we own or can buy, and that is a hard one to shake off.

If you're really brave and ready to turn this around, let someone else look at your finances and help you cut back. They might cut your satellite TV and Starbucks coffee, so be prepared. But this is a great way to get an objective look at how to get yourself out of this situation (and probably, ouch, you will see signs of how you got into it in the first place).

CHANGE: Okay, are you ready to take the first step? I know you can do it. Buckle down and find a way to bring your financial problems into a good balance again (or for the first time). Don't think of it as a loss, but as a gain! You may not be able to go out to dinner with your friends for a while like you used to, but you will be shocked at the influence you will have if you walk through this with a great attitude!

One afternoon I was going to lunch with a friend. We would do this about once a month, but this time instead of ordering my usual high-fat, crazy-carb meal, I got something light and simple. She asked me about it and I explained that I was trying to lose weight and get my diet back on a healthy track. She was so disappointed and said to me, "I am so sorry you can't eat what you want. This is going to be awful for you."

I didn't skip a beat before replying, "Actually, I *can* eat anything I want. I choose not to and I am completely happy knowing I am respecting myself and taking good care of what God has given me."

Sadly she didn't understand, and as you can imagine, she doesn't ask me to lunch anymore.

Not everyone will get on board with your new lifestyle, and that's got to be okay with you. You don't want to live to impress people or make them happy. You live to please God, and He wants you to have financial freedom. Not riches and hot cars. That is not what freedom looks like!

Move ahead with confidence that each step you take today will be one that gets you closer to the end of money arguments and bank foreclosures. You will be amazed at what God will do when you begin this new adventure with gratitude for everything you have and the wisdom to undo the mess you've made.

ENDURE: If you're like us, enduring the financial struggle will probably take years. In my life the length of time it took to get myself out of financial trouble is what stops me now from descending into it again. I know how hard it is to get out of debt; I don't ever want to go through that again. You can pray all you want for an inheritance, but it won't make any difference in how you think. The people who win the lottery almost always go broke again, and worse. The money that is quickly earned does not teach you a lesson until afterward. And those are *hard* lessons, my friend!

GIVING

I left this section for the end because to me it is the most important. It's about giving, sharing, being generous. This is a beautiful expression of love and support for someone and you don't want to miss the blessings that come from giving out of your own need.

Giving is easier for some people than others, but we all need to be doing what we can financially to support our friends, our churches, those in need, and our communities. This is the money that, when you give it away, goes further than any other money you spend. You do it out of pure love and sacrifice, and the blessings you will receive are not even in your imagination. You get so much more out of it than the recipient of your gifts.

Some of us tend to want to give too much. I am constantly asking my husband, "Honey, can I give fifty dollars to this person for their adoption/medical bills/what-have-you?" He likes to stick to our allotted amount of giving, and this has been wise. I appreciate his care and protection for our family while he prays about our family's giving. I urge you to put in place a policy that you have to both agree before you give outside of your regular, predetermined amount. James and I have a column in our budget for giving, and unless God moves us both (which He definitely does from time to time), we stay with it.

You always want to be reaching outside of yourself and helping others. Sometimes it's through money; sometimes it's through other ways. Please don't let the weight of financial burdens ever stop you from doing for others. There's no better cure for the money blues than to serve someone else.

ASSIGNMENT

You might have expected the little assignment at the end here to be something like (in a deep voice) "Write down all of your bills and how much you make, and do some serious math!" But no, you can figure that out by yourself.

I want to encourage you to make a different kind of list. I want this to inspire you to stick to your goals and keep at the changes you want to make. I want you to believe in yourself as I believe in you! So tell me, what are three things you would do if you had complete financial freedom? Make it big, no holds barred.

Think of things that would be beyond you right now and how much they would cost. Trips, cars, clothes, savings, what is your dream? Write down those costs, and keep them where you can see them. Anytime you are tempted to veer from your plan, look at your list as a reminder that you can get those things with perseverance.

What are your dreams for your life that are being held back by finances? As long as you keep them fairly realistic, you can accomplish them! I know it!

10

TAMING THE TONGUE

*Let no corrupting talk come out of your mouths, but
only such as is good for building up, as fits the occasion,
that it may give grace to those who hear.*

Ephesians 4:29

NAILS IN THE FENCE
(AUTHOR UNKNOWN)

There once was a little boy who had a bad temper. His father gave
him a bag of nails and told him that every time he lost his temper,
he must hammer a nail into the back of the fence. The first day the
boy had driven thirty-seven nails into the fence. Over the next few
weeks, as the boy learned to control his anger, the number of nails
hammered daily gradually dwindled. He discovered it was easier to
hold his temper than to drive those nails into the fence.

Eventually, the day came when the boy didn't lose his temper
at all. He told his father about it and the father suggested that the
boy now pull out one nail for each day that he was able to hold his
temper. The days passed and the young boy was finally able to tell
his father that all the nails were gone.

The father took his son by the hand and led him to the fence.
He said, "You have done well, my son, but look at the holes in the
fence. The fence will never be the same. When you say things in

anger, they leave scars just like these. You can put a knife in a man and draw it out. It won't matter how many times you say I'm sorry; the wound is still there."

The little boy then understood how powerful his words were. He looked up at his father and said, "I hope you can forgive me, Father, for the holes I put in you."

"Of course I can," said the father.

This simple story had a great effect on me when I first heard it. After reading it, I saw my words differently. Was I driving nails in when I criticized my children? Could I deliver my message differently so as not to leave so many scars?

I found that just thinking about it caused me to speak more softly and deliberately. I am sure I have left holes, but thank God He can fill them!

JUST TWO INCHES

A mouth is such a small thing—just a few inches of space in the head. But oh, can it create trouble! That old saying "Sticks and stones may break my bones but words can never hurt me" is baloney! Give me a broken bone over a broken heart any day! The words we speak have the power to change the world. Words are lessons, encouragement, story sharers, heart warmers, love expressers, lifters, and light. But they can also be bullies, hate spreaders, pain deliverers, confusers, bitter pills, dark holes, and life drainers. Or they may fall somewhere in between with carelessness, thoughtlessness, or just lack of education.

But the mouth, while it is small compared to the rest of the body, represents more than itself. It is the reflector of what is in the heart. We can't hide who we are because it comes pouring out through our words. I sometimes find myself thinking that I can just pretend to like someone or be selfless, but it doesn't work. My mouth will reveal my secret. Luke 6:45 says, "The good person out of the good treasure of his heart produces good, and the evil person out of his evil treasure produces evil, for out of the abundance of the heart his mouth speaks."

Your wisdom, your treasure, your truthfulness all lie in your heart, and your mouth is just the, well, mouthpiece. Noah Webster in 1828 defined *mouthpiece* as "one who delivers the opinions of others." Yep, that's what your words do. They deliver the opinion of your heart. If you want to change the way you share and encourage and communicate, you have to change your heart.

In a great little book called *Lord, Change My Attitude*, James MacDonald wrote:

> As a pastor, I frequently hear people say, "I just don't seem to be able to find any friends …" or "Every time I try to find friends …" And before they're three sentences into their sad story, you just want to say, "Do you know what? It's your attitude! It's your critical, negative, faultfinding attitude. Do you know why you're alone? They're not into your attitude."[1]

It is wise to learn to hold back those thoughts of hatred or criticism. We all have moments when we want to slam someone for their position or actions. When I get rudely cut off in traffic, I have to stop myself from reacting hatefully. It's our nature! But what makes us human is our ability to stop ourselves from acting on our every natural reaction. If someone hits me, my animal instinct is to either run or hit the person back. But I actually have other choices that the animal kingdom doesn't. I can show kindness. I can forgive.

If caring about someone else is not enough to stop you, or if by some sad misconception you actually believe that another person deserves to be lashed at, then hopefully knowing what it will do to you can help you let it go completely.

I THINK I HAVE MADE A BIG MISTAKE

Our words can get us in big trouble. If I had a nickel for every time I regretted my words the very moment they came out of my mouth, I would be able to buy a nice apartment overlooking Central Park. Sadly, no one is paying me for my poor speech.

Look, you will make mistakes, you will say the wrong thing, you will hurt people's feelings, and you will have regrets. Part of maturing is seeing when you mess up and apologizing. It doesn't always fix a problem, but it's a start. You can't control whether the other person will forgive you, but you can be repentant and learn from it.

I am the *queen* of saying the wrong thing. Often, it's not even my heart that is the problem but my lack of tact. I don't think long enough before I speak, and consequently, I say something rude or accidentally hurtful. I say "accidentally" because it usually is a genuine mistake on my part. As I have gotten older, learned to be less opinionated and more loving, and developed a deeper love for the people God puts in my life and concern for their well-being, I am rarely actually lashing out.

To add to it, I sometimes don't realize I have hurt someone until days (or months) later, after they have let it stew and begun to build a dislike toward me. By the time I discover the problem, it has gotten huge and I am the bad guy. If you haven't been able to tell from reading this book, I have quite a bit of experience with this particular problem.

But here's the truth, straight from this expert of saying the wrong thing: you are going to mess up. When you realize it, be humble, apologize, try to make it right if you can, then move on. Whether the other person forgives you is not a prerequisite to forgiving yourself. You know you're sorry, you meant it when you apologized, you will try not to do it again, and that's all you can do.

Don't beat yourself up over a mistake!

FRIENDS DON'T LET FRIENDS TALK TRASH

One area we have got to get a hold of when it comes to the mouth is (cue dreaded music) gossip.

Gossip in this case is tearing down other people, talking about them in ways you wouldn't if they were with you, and exposing their private information, which typically is unconfirmed information, twisted to make a point. It betrays a confidence, stirs up dissension, and spreads lies. No good ever comes from gossiping.

There is something inside of us (it's called sin) that makes us want to lift ourselves above other people. We find their flaws, either real or imagined, and we make sure the rest of the world can see them. We cut them up and serve them on a platter to anyone who will stop long enough to listen.

Karen Ehman has a great book on this subject called *Keep It Shut*. She wrote:

> I'd rather be known for dishing up a hearty batch of my famous cheesy corn chowder than for stirring up a bunch of drama in my close circle of friends. If relationships are damaged and feelings are wounded, do we want our words to be the cause? And just knowing that the Bible uses the word *perverse* to describe such a person should make us stop and think the next time we are tempted to participate in gossip.[2]

If you find yourself tempted to gossip, you have to treat it like any other sin. You must ask God's forgiveness and repent. Then keep asking and giving it to Him over and over again. One thing I know for sure is that He wants to help you stop gossiping. He makes it abundantly clear that it is wrong, and He wouldn't do that if there was no solution.

Gossips tend to be, naturally, drawn to other gossips. If your friends are willing to listen to this kind of talk, then you can be sure that they are willing to talk the same about you behind your back. If this is a struggle for you, it's time to seek out people who won't listen to your gossip. Find someone you admire and spend more time with her, even if it's only serving beside her in the church kitchen or saving her a seat at your kids' basketball game.

Remember that sometimes it is necessary to mention another person in conversation. It's not necessarily gossip to say her name. But ask yourself these three things before you do:

1. Am I revealing a secret or sharing something she wouldn't want shared?

2. Am I a part of the problem? Or can I be a part of the solution? If not, don't discuss it.

3. Can I keep the focus on how to work on my own issues and not on hers? If I can't keep the focus on myself, I need to stop talking about it.

And those friends that you gossip with now, be prepared to lose them when you quit gossiping. Once you stop playing the game of tearing other people down, they won't want to hang out with you anymore. You will likely become their next target. Forgive them now.

I have carefully chosen my dearest friends to be people who would not let me gossip if I wanted to. Occasionally when we need to talk about a problem we are having with another person, we will say, "I only want to tell you my problem. Please stop me if it turns to gossip, because I don't want to do that." And I have definitely been stopped. It is so, so easy to lose sight of being careful when you're just chatting with a close friend!

THERE'S A TIME FOR EVERYTHING

We do still have to talk sometimes. We can't walk around like we have duct tape covering our mouths, so where's the line? How do we know when to speak up? After all, there are injustices in the world and we aren't always called to keep our mouths shut. When is the time to say something? Where does controlling the tongue fall into the definition of righteous anger?

The example of this in Scripture is when Jesus went into the temple and found people selling sheep and oxen and He turned the tables over and said, "Is it not written, 'My house shall be called a house of prayer for all the nations'? But you have made it a den of robbers" (Mark 11:17). We see Him here tossing the wares to the ground and repeating the scriptures to explain His actions. Jesus showed some evidence of sternness (1:43) and indignance (10:14). If Christ did these things, then we can be sure that it was done in love.

I noticed as I studied these examples that He never once said anything to build a gang of defenders, but always pointed back to the Father and His wisdom. He taught with justice, corrected with wisdom, and gave witness to the mercy of God. Even His anger served to point people to God, not just make them angry with Him.

When you determine that an occasion calls for a bit of speaking out, check your heart to be sure you are promoting God's agenda and not your own. If something makes you feel bad, is it because of childhood baggage and hard life experiences? Or because God says that it's wrong? One good rule of thumb is to wait until your emotional anger subsides before you actually speak. If it is just emotion, then you probably don't need to say it. If it is wisdom and righteousness, then you will be able to speak with truth and gentleness.

HOW WILL I CHANGE?

If you've been reading through this chapter thinking, *Uh-oh. I gotta lotta work to do!* then you are not alone. Being wise with your tongue is a lifelong effort. If you realize you have not been paying enough attention and maybe crashed and burned a few times lately, it's okay. Start now.

BEGIN: No time like the present. In fact, if you have seen yourself even slightly in some of these scenarios, then you won't be able to escape it now. You're stuck with a new conviction. You'll thank me later.

ASSESS: How bad is it? Are you finding yourself reaching for the phone every time you hear a new rumor? Do you grab your girlfriend at church and pull her to the back to be sure she has heard what happened? Do you feel a little thrill anytime someone says to you, "I shouldn't be telling you this, but ..."? These are signs that you have issues that need dealing with. If you allow a friend to tell you someone else's secret, you need to set about putting a stop to that. Believe me; it's hard at first to tell someone that you won't discuss their rumors. It feels awkward, especially if it has been the core of your friendship until then. But it is so, so worth it!

LEARN: The Bible has so much to say on this subject that it is clearly a problem! If God needs to tell us over and over to stop spreading lies and guard our tongues, then we must really need to hear it. I know I do. How many times do I have to be told before I will learn? Oh, probably as many as there are grains of sand. I'm a stubborn old gal. Here are a couple of my favorite verses to inspire me to be careful about what I say:

- "I tell you, on the day of judgment people will give account for every careless word they speak, for by your words you will be justified, and by your words you will be condemned" (Matt. 12:36–37).
- "If anyone thinks he is religious and does not bridle his tongue but deceives his heart, this person's religion is worthless" (James 1:26).

ACCOUNT: How do we measure taming our tongues? It's easy. Count how many times a day you want to say something you shouldn't, then work to reduce that number by half. Then half that, and so on, until you have broken the habit. Pay attention to how strong the urge is and try to weaken it by feeding it with good thoughts when it strikes. The big feeling of "I want to tell someone this!" can be calmed with a few worship songs and prayers. You could even tell yourself to pray for the person who is the subject of your attention instead of talking about or openly criticizing him or her.

NOTIFY: Gossiping is a habit in many of us, and habits are hard to break! You might consider letting everyone know that you have made this a new goal. This is not to try to change anyone else, but to let them know you really want to make some changes for yourself.

Remember also, when you tell someone that you are going to stop gossiping, she may feel defensive. It is not an easy conversation, so be clear you're not accusing her of anything but only trying to work on what God is convicting you of.

And of course, through prayer, invite the Holy Spirit to help you too. He is always with you and can touch your heart and remind you to stop.

CHANGE: Here you go; you're ready for a whole new you. The key here is to *work on your heart*! What goes in is what comes out. Fill your eyes and ears with good things, like books that encourage you and music that points to God. If you tend to criticize others, look at what you can feed your heart to stop that. Are you letting people spread critical thoughts to you or are you spending too much time on social media? Step away and spend that time on something else.

This is the time for you to make your plan. You may need to just go cold turkey on the gossip until you get a better feel for what is damaging and what is necessary. You will be shocked at how many times a day you are tempted when you quit completely.

If you are trying to stop saying mean things to your husband, change your heart attitude toward him. Fill your thoughts with ways you can bless him, and think of five words you can use instead of the ones you tend to fall back on. You might even practice in the mirror so you're ready with a smile and a kind word.

ENDURE: Have patience with yourself. As long as you are making the changes, don't worry if you slip up once in a while without thinking. Just apologize, acknowledge that you messed up, and move on. One thing that may take time here is the other person's willingness to change with you. They have their own bad habits and hurts, and they might not have read this book. Give them room to get used to the new you, and forgive them of their slowness to accept it.

It takes courage to change the way you communicate. Your relationships are built on who you are now, and it will be a rebuilding, of sorts, to transform this part of your thought process and behavior. The things you say affect everything else around you. That should offer you hope because you can no doubt see the effects of your word choices on the lives of those around you. That means you can have a new effect. But it also can be scary because some people will reject you once you stop joining their insecure fun. Don't ever let the fear of losing someone convince you to stop improving yourself. Pray for them, love them, don't try to change them. But *you* be who you are called to be no matter what!

As Karen Ehman said, "Yes, the tongue has power. Words can hurt. Sting, destroy, devastate. Or words can heal, build up, encourage, and cheer. How are you going to wield your power?"[3]

ASSIGNMENT

Make a list of verses that inspire you to pay attention to the words you say. Now, choose one and try to memorize it. Believe me; I know this is tough because I sometimes feel like my brain won't retain new information anymore. Oh sure, I can remember all the words to "Hopelessly Devoted to You" from 1978, but don't ask me to remember what I studied in my Bible study last week. If you're like me, this will take effort, but I won't ask you to do anything I am not willing to do. Let's bury these in our hearts!

MOODS: YEP, I'M GOING THERE

And the Lord's servant must not be quarrelsome but
kind to everyone, able to teach, patiently enduring
evil, correcting his opponents with gentleness.

2 Timothy 2:24–25

GREEN EGGS, NO HAM

We live on a small hobby farm and have dabbled in raising goats, horses, chickens, rabbits, and even a cow. We really aren't talented in this area. Once when one of our goats was having trouble giving birth, we got out all of our books about small farms, set up some plastic lawn chairs behind the goat, and sat there looking up goat-birth troubleshooting while she pushed.

Those babies did eventually come out, but it wasn't thanks to us.

Our chickens are another constant learning process. Now that I've had them for a dozen years, I pretty much have the hang of it, at least enough to keep them alive and laying eggs. But in the beginning, as with the goats, I got some books and started reading. I decided to want chickens that lay blue and green eggs. I had visions of blowing out the insides of the eggs and making crafts with the gorgeous shells. So I researched which kind of chickens I needed and went to the nearest feed store to order them. They told me that they didn't sell chickens but that if I went to the next small town a lady at that feed store specializes in "them fancy chickens."

I found the place, way off the beaten path, and asked the lady about the chickens I wanted. I felt slightly overdressed, mainly because I was not covered in animal poop and hay like all the other people in there. We got the chickens ordered, and she told me to come back in exactly one week to pick up my chicks. I was pretty excited.

Exactly one week later I drove to the hard-to-find feed store and walked in to get my chicks. The woman took one look at me and started yelling, "You were supposed to be here yesterday! I told you one week and now I have had to be watchin' after them chicks all night!"

I was stunned. I really thought I had the right day. I apologized, and as she grabbed my chicks out of the cage and shoved them into a brown paper sack, I asked if there was anything I could do to make it up to her. She whipped around and screamed in my face, "YOU CAN GET YERSELF OUTTA HERE AND NEVER COME BACK!"

I was seconds away from bursting into tears. I knew that wouldn't help matters at all, considering this woman with hard lines around her eyes and skin as thick as leather probably had not cried since 1967.

So I prayed as I felt her angry breath in my face.

"Ma'am," I told her, "I apologize from the bottom of my heart. I misunderstood the day and I will not come back if that is what you want. But I hope you know that I really appreciate you letting me get my chicks here and I am just nothing but grateful for you taking such good care of them."

She stood there, stone faced, and finally stepped to the register and took my money.

I really wanted to react. I wanted to either cry or start yelling back at her. Two can play at that game, lady. But I didn't.

As I unlocked my car and held the bag of peeping chicks in my hand, a man in coveralls and a pitchfork started walking toward me. *This is it, Lord. I am going to die right here in this parking lot with a bag of chickens in my hand,* I thought.

Thankfully, he didn't kill me with his pitchfork. Instead, he started talking to me.

"Lady," he said, "I never saw anyone just take it like that. Good fer you. She oughtta be feelin' pretty embarrassed about now. You didn't do nothin' wrong. You come on back anytime ya feel like it."

Well, I never did go back, but I was sure glad I held my emotions close and didn't react to the shock of her yelling. Your reactions have an effect on other people, even those just watching!

And I sure did enjoy my blue and green eggs!

EMOTIONS AREN'T FOR THE WEAK

As women, we are rich with hormones and emotions and mood swings and fears we don't know what to do with. We can be fine one minute and the next we are so far out of balance it feels impossible to change. The lion in the jungle is more predictable than we are.

The smallest thing can make me cry. Out of nowhere.

Feelings can seem so real that we quickly make decisions based on them. And they are real for a minute. Right now I might be frustrated. But if I say, "I am so frustrated with my friend not returning my things that I am going to call her up and tell her I want my books back that I loaned her last week!" and then I call her and find out she is having a rough day, I will instantly feel sorry for her and decide to let her keep the books. Then I will get off the phone and remember she also borrowed my cookbook with the recipe I planned to use tonight and I'm frustrated again.

We go 'round and 'round with our emotions. They can be rooted in circumstances, hormones, fear, stress, or even our diet. I know for me, when I change my diet and make it healthier, I don't struggle as much with mood swings.

I want to be crystal clear right from the start that I am talking about only simple cases of emotional imbalances. A mental illness or clinical depression is a whole different situation and must be handled by a professional. Please, if you're reading through this and realize you are beyond the scope of the simple balance ideas that I am sharing, seek counsel from a medical professional.

I KEEP MY FEAR IN A SUITCASE

So often, even though we don't realize it, our mood swings come from a place of fear. I react to something happening that threatens my sense of safety or comfort. In the moment it seems as though I am fussing because my husband used my favorite mug to hold his fingernail clippings ... again. But what is really upsetting me? The mug, while gross, can be washed. I am afraid of not being respected. I am hurt because that mug reminds me of my grandmother and it's been mine since I was a little girl—all kinds of emotions wrapped around that cup. It's the baggage of a lifetime of fear of not being cared for or losing something I have worked for and might not have again. It's a heap o' junk I carry around with me.

Fear is one of those things that God clearly tells us is wrong: "Fear not, for I am with you" (Isa. 41:10). But boy, oh boy, I think we all struggle with this one. He is right, of course. He is God! If He says it, then we should believe it with no reservations. But it is so easy to slip into the trap, and then our emotions get involved, and before we know it we are caught between being afraid and all the pain from our past.

Living in fear is definitely a time to look at your balance. Do you see it for what it is? Can you evaluate the problem objectively? Do you need someone to hold you accountable and give you assurance? Have you checked the Bible for comfort and truth?

Recognizing your fear and admitting it to someone is the start to a path of health with your emotions. Embrace the freedom and let go of past hurts. No matter what your history is, it is over. God wants you to use the pain to let Him do miracles in you and to glorify Him.

MEET FEAR'S COUSIN, ANXIETY

I want to say again that in this book I am not addressing severe cases of emotional imbalance or actual illnesses. There are people with straight-up clinical anxiety. Those precious souls can still have victory, but if you need help for a more acute issue, I beg you to find it. Everyone reading this, please stop and pray for someone with anxiety or depression. It is a very hard place to be.

For those of us just trying to manage the less acute version, known as "trying to be supermom and not making it," there is also hope. Hormones too can cause anxiety; I dealt with that after each baby. It goes away, thankfully.

Webster's 1828 defines *anxiety* as "concern or solicitude respecting some event, future or uncertain, which disturbs the mind and keeps it in a state of painful uneasiness."

"Painful uneasiness," what a great description. Like fear, the Bible says not to be anxious about anything but to give it to God in prayer. When we break anxiety down into pain, it makes it easier to balance. Emotional pain needs aid, like prayer and praise. Uneasiness needs rest and comfort.

We have to be prepared for when anxiety hits, because the moment it happens, it's too late to make decisions. Like hot flashes, you have about a two-second warning and then you are on fire and no other woman will blame you if you strip down to your skivvies and jump in the kiddie pool. The moment you feel it coming, have a signal ready for your family. They also need to brace themselves for your sudden change in attitude.

Stop what you're doing and take some long, slow breaths. Then pray and ask God to guide you through the difficulty. Find some verses about anxiety, and post them around the house with chalk art or printed cards or just Post-it notes. I know it seems overly simple, but according to the Bible, His yoke is easy and His burden is light (Matt. 11:28–30).

ARE YOU JUST MAD?

When we were young and dreamed of having a husband and kids, we didn't picture ourselves being mad all the time. But we get worn down, and eventually we see ourselves turning into the Incredible Hulk. Years of spills and apathy and laziness and dis-respect and being used as a milk machine can whittle you down to a one-woman anger show.

Gary Chapman wrote a great book about anger called *Anger: Handling a Powerful Emotion in a Healthy Way*. He said, "In all anger there is first a provoking event; second, an interpretation of that event; and third, the rising emotion of anger. Physiological changes take place in the body, and we are ready for action. All of this occurs whether the anger is definitive or distorted. But if we are to have a wise response to anger, we must first discern whether that anger is based upon actual wrongdoing. This requires time and thought."[1]

When you're dealing with anger, take it apart until you can see each response separately. From the time the trigger happens until you explode, how many steps are there? Think about how you got there. Look at what the trigger was and if your reaction was appropriate or if you were really reacting to years of being upset all rolled into this moment.

Moms, our anger must be dealt with if we want to raise emotionally healthy children. This is for you. Become aware of what leads you down the path of just being mad, and deal with it.

Start with what you actually have a right to. Your family doesn't owe you a perfect life. You are servant, not master. I have no doubt that you get treated poorly occasionally and they only think of themselves. I'll bet you do that to them sometimes too. This is what life together looks like, and if you are mad about it, then we need to work on some things.

SO LET'S TALK DEPRESSION

Depression is so prevalent today. The term is used to cover a huge range of issues, from feeling blue to a clinical diagnosis. If you're dealing with clinical depression, please see someone who is trained to help. I care too much about you to let another minute go by without suggesting that you seek attention. I can't give you medical advice, so keep reading and believe there is hope, and believe that you are worth the effort to talk to a professional.

The depression I want to discuss could be better described as the blues, feeling down, struggling with joy. I know I have felt all of those things at different times, and that makes me your biggest cheerleader! You can't go through feeling unexplainably low and not have sympathy for anyone else who is going through the same thing.

You do not need to be ashamed of being depressed. People get turned off by someone who is down all the time, so we try to hide it. But your real friends will understand and hopefully try to help. Be grateful that, no matter how fumbling, they want to help. People who think they can just bring you chocolate to make it all better don't get it. Just love 'em (and eat the chocolate, of course).

There's a way to share your burden without being a drag on the people around you. You can talk about it humbly, as if you know it's your emotions that are the issue and not the things you really want to complain about. It is when you start criticizing others as if they caused your problems, blaming your hard time on everyone but yourself, or gossiping that it goes very wrong. Do that and eventually you will lose friends and be left thinking everyone around you is a jerk, when in reality they just felt that they couldn't help you. It feeds itself, because then you are disappointed and hurt and become more depressed.

When you are in a low place, one way to find balance is to be aware that your sadness is most of the cause of your pain. Sure, someone treated you badly or there might be a reason for your struggle, but there is good all around you. And if you aren't seeing it, then you need to make some inner changes. It's not easy, and you may not be able to do it quickly, but at least recognizing it will set you on the path to freedom.

GOD HAS AN IDEA

God is not silent on the subject of fear, depression, or moodiness. One of my favorites is Proverbs 12:25: "Anxiety in a man's heart weighs him down, but a good word makes him glad." If it was something we couldn't control, then He would just say things like, "Good luck, buddy. You're gonna need it."

He wants us to give our cares over to Him. When we explode at the kids for the tenth time today, He is ready to release us. When we are feeling like nothing will ever get better and want to bury the pain in ice cream, He offers a better solution.

A balanced, healthy emotional core is possible for you, even if you feel like you struggle more than most. You can have that genuine, Spirit-led kind of joy that you see others experiencing. It is there for the asking, even though sometimes you have to work at it.

God is handling every problem in your life right this second, and in the future He has it under control and is preparing you for whatever comes. He provides everything you need (notice I didn't say "want," which is a bummer, but He knows best).

You can trust Him with all of your mistakes; He will use them for your good. When you act ugly, apologize. Mean it and do better next time. Trusting God for all of your needs, emotional or otherwise, is the key to real joy. It doesn't come from your problems going away, but from your hope drawing near. Hope and believe that He knows how you are feeling and cares about the deepest places in your heart.

CALGON, TAKE ME AWAY!

In normal, everyday life there is stress. We live in a go-go-go society where all moms are pressured to live in Pinterest-worthy houses and have kids' birthday parties that could be featured in magazines. I mean, if you don't craft a perfect bow on your handmade Christmas gifts, then you are clearly not measuring up.

The pressure today to keep up with social media and have a picture-worthy dinner on the table is too much, y'all. We are stressing ourselves out over things that are not important. If you really like a well-plated meal, then hoorah for you! But I just want my ketchup not to touch my fries until I am good and ready to eat them.

I love social media; I really do. But being online all day long is not good for anyone and it adds not only to our stress but also to our mood problems. I love my modern kitchen, but it's healthy for our family to cook outside occasionally and just be together without the speed of electricity. I'm not suggesting we all go Amish and start riding around in buggies. I just want to remind us (myself included) that much of what is keeping us out of balance could be eliminated, or at least reduced.

There are real pressures. There are sick kids and bills to be paid and painful relationships, and too many more to name. Those are the things that will throw off anyone, but not someone calling you names on Facebook. That's just immaturity, and your maturity gives you the power of ignoring it and not letting it keep you from joy and well-being.

If you're dealing with stress that is affecting your moods, remember that God gave us stress as a natural way to protect us. We have an instinct to escape when we get stressed, which we don't generally need to do, so we are stuck in that place and can't get away from it. It takes an act of will and purpose to let go of stress and let God show us how to really, truly relax.

EMOTIONS ARE A GIFT

Those things, those emotions that cause us so much trouble, are really an amazing, beautiful gift! Even the negative feelings are a blessing:

- Happiness gives us a sense of well-being and confidence.
- Thankfulness reminds us to see what God and others have done for us.
- Disgust makes us avoid things that are not good for us.
- Anger propels us to fight when necessary.
- Excitement gives us a boost of energy necessary to accomplish a task.
- Nervousness forces us to focus all of our energy on the task at hand.
- Embarrassment stops us from doing something foolish.
- Fear keeps us out of harm's way.

There are, of course, many other emotions. Didn't you see *Inside Out*? There are emotions, memories, and even a stuffed animal elephant with a wagon. Duh.

Anger is the number one thing moms talk to me about. They struggle with their anger toward their kids, then feel guilty for being so mean. Even anger, in its place, has a God-given purpose. It's just not meant for things like unfinished chores and kids who move too slowly. In those instances we need to bring out other emotions, such as calmness and confidence. Calm when things aren't going the way you want, and confidence that with some effort you could make some changes in the situation.

We get so wrapped up (and I am talking to myself here!) in how we want things to go that we forget there are other people involved. Our kids may be careless and slow and even lazy, but do they deserve to be screamed at and treated like their feelings don't matter at all? I hope your answer was no.

In *Unglued*, Lysa TerKeurst said it like this:

> God gave us emotions. Emotions allow us to feel as we experience life. Because we feel, we connect. We share laughter and know the gift of empathy. Our emotions are what enable us to drink deeply from love and treasure it. And yes, we also experience difficult emotions such as sadness, fear, shame, and anger. But might these be important as well? Just as touching a hot stove signals our hand to pull back, might

our hot emotions be alerting us to potential danger?[2]

It's time to take back our moods and claim victory over our painful uneasiness. Even though there will always be good days and bad, the extreme problems can be a thing of the past.

Emotional health is ready and waiting for you!

BALANCE

BEGIN: Are you ready to become a person who has conquered the uncontrolled moods and unpredictable reactions? I know I want to be a person who can be counted on to react to difficulties in a positive way.

This is a hard one because we are pretty connected to our feelings. But you will still have feelings, just better ones. I'm going to be brutally honest; this can be like quitting smoking—it might feel like you're dying. If you have spent a lot of time blowing up whenever the mood struck you, then you will need time to relearn how to react, and like a baby learning to walk, you will take some tumbles.

Just start and let the Holy Spirit wash His peace over you every time you feel like you can't control yourself.

ASSESS: Take a hard look at yourself the next time you are in a crisis mood situation. Stop and think, *What led me here?* Be real and don't accept a shallow answer like blaming another person or saying you couldn't help it. You can always help your actions.

Emotions are tricky. They communicate to us, but what they say is not always true. Be sure you are making your decisions based on pure fact.

Check your diet; are you eating too much junk? That can seriously affect your moods! How's your sleep? Studies have shown that lack of sleep can cause depression, anxiety, aging, and forgetfulness. Is your schedule too full, or are you feeling unnecessary pressures? If your job is causing stress or you have a difficult child, you may not be able to change those circumstances, but identifying them will help. I am a natural-remedy nut and love my essential oils and vitamins for getting me through a rough emotional time.

When you're evaluating where you have gotten off balance, consider where you are making emotional decisions. Step back and see your reactions from a distance. How would it look to you if someone else were responding this way?

I remember one year a good friend of mine had a birthday party for her daughter and didn't invite my daughter, who was the same age. Our kids were friends and several mutual friends were going, so when I heard about it from someone else, I was hurt. I thought maybe she forgot to invite us so I tried to subtly probe. "Hey, what are y'all doing next Thursday afternoon? Anything fun?"

"Nope, nothing really," she said.

What? She just lied to me! Really, I know it's a kid birthday party, but I was so hurt.

I wanted to jump in and cry and tell her how hurt I was, but I knew better than to react emotionally. So I talked with my husband about it. He reminded me that while it hurt my feelings, she had a right to invite whoever she wanted to her party and there were probably circumstances I didn't know about. If I wanted to continue the friendship, I needed to get over it and be kind about it.

Ugh. Blargh.

But that was exactly what I did. Oh sure, I kind of fumed for a while, which frankly revealed a level of immaturity in me that I was frustrated with. I wanted to be the kind of person who didn't get her panties in a wad because my daughter wasn't invited to a party. I knew it didn't really matter. But I got to really see some ugly stuff in my heart, and because I hadn't brought it up to my friend, I was able to take some time to process it.

Years later she told me that she wanted to apologize for something that had happened in the past. She had felt badly for a long time about lying to me one day, and of course I knew exactly what she meant; but I just smiled and listened.

She said her daughter had a party and they had very little money for food or games, so they made a deal with the girl that she could have only three friends over and that would afford them to make it nicer than a large party. Their financial struggles were something they were trying to keep hidden and those few years for her were a nightmare that she regrets keeping hidden. She didn't know what to do, so she lied to me and several other friends about the party because she was embarrassed and thought we would try to fix it somehow. I was the only friend who didn't get mad at her about it; in fact, she was never really sure if I even knew about it or not. The other two women were long gone from her life over that conflict. But she and I are good friends even now.

I could tell you story after story of how not reacting to my emotions but instead taking a truthful look at what is happening has saved my bacon. Left to myself I would probably be fighting with everyone, but God used wisdom and selflessness (not mine, but His) to grow me up.

LEARN: Speaking of God, He created our emotions and doesn't want us to ignore them. He also knew that balancing feelings and fact would be hard, so He gave us lots of help in His Word. Here are a couple of my favorite verses, but go look for yourself and you will find many that speak directly to your heart.

- "A fool gives full vent to his spirit, but a wise man quietly holds it back" (Prov. 29:11).
- "Do not be conformed to this world, but be transformed by the renewal of your mind, that by testing you may discern what is the will of God, what is good and acceptable and perfect" (Rom. 12:2).

What is renewal of the mind? It is recognizing that our minds, thoughts, and emotions without God have no good in them. We need Christ to transform us. Being renewed is believing that God gives us everything we need, letting go of our own expectations, and fully embracing His place in our lives. It is freedom from the bondage of being controlled by our own ideas, emotions, and failings.

When you find verses that speak to you, read all around them instead of just pulling out one and using it out of its intended context. Try not to prove your own point, and see what God has to say with an objective eye.

ACCOUNT: How do you measure emotional problems? Using width and breadth is one way. How damaging is your response? Can you reduce that in some way, little by little, until it's gone? Or measure with time: How often do you respond in out-of-controlled ways? Think of how often you do that, and ask God to give you wisdom to reduce the amount. Pay attention so you will know if what you are doing is working!

NOTIFY: Find people who you know have conquered their emotional baggage, and ask them for help. There is nothing like hard experience to teach love and compassion. If you are struggling with balance emotionally, you need a person who understands but will not let you use excuses that stop you from growing.

This will be painful. It's not easy to hear that you did damage to your kids or that you are part of destroying your marriage. But if you really want to get yourself on a path to emotional wellness, you need to find someone who will lovingly tell you the truth.

No matter how big or small your issue, do not try to do this alone!

CHANGE: Okay, friend, here we go. It's time to change the course of what you are doing to yourself and your family.

As the Boy Scouts say, be prepared. You will get all pumped to be cheerful or easygoing, and then *bam*! One of your kids has a meltdown about eating the breakfast casserole you so brilliantly prepared ahead of time and you are right back to square one. Or are you? You are now aware, with goals, of areas you need to work on. You are willing to take responsibility for your actions and be humble when you mess up. You may not react how you want to on day 1 (or 2 or 25), but you have made changes.

Again from Lysa's great book *Unglued*, we read: "When someone else's actions or statements threaten to pull me into a bad place, I have a choice. I do. It may not feel like it. In fact, it may feel like I am a slave to my feelings—but I'm not. Remember, feelings are indicators, not dictators. They can indicate there is a situation I need to deal with, but they shouldn't dictate how I react. I have a choice."[3]

Make a plan, keep evaluating, use your skills, and you can do this!

ENDURE: Struggles with emotions go back to the days when the cavemen hit the women over the head with clubs and dragged them into the cave. Every Bible story has an element of an out-of-balance emotional situation. David lusted, Cain was jealous, Paul had many conflicts.

We don't get where we want to be instantly. If you're looking for God to perform a miracle and just take your problems from you, you are looking for the wrong miracle. The miracle did happen. He created you and gave you tools to handle your problems, people who love you, a place to live, food, and His Word as a guide. You aren't without miracles, my friend. You just need to see them.

Be patient with yourself as you learn new ways to respond and grow. When you feel as though you're going backward, return to the BALANCE list, reignite your determination, and find new ideas.

Like ripples in the water, when you start to get victory over your emotional battles, the people around you will be affected. Your kids will trust you more, which will release some potential baggage they carry. Your friendships will be richer, and your marriage will grow stronger.

I know I say this at the end of almost every chapter, but it's because I believe it so deeply that I want to shout it over and over: *you can do this!*

ASSIGNMENT

Identify the emotion that you struggle with most. Is it fear? Or pride? Or anger? Then look up verses about it. Write down one or two that really resonate with you, or if none speak to you, then just pick one. God will use it. Now read it every morning, out loud, when you're getting dressed. Let's see what God will do with it!

12

MISCELLANEOUS

*Not that I am speaking of being in need, for I have
learned in whatever situation I am to be content.*

Philippians 4:11

WOMEN ARE COMPLICATED

There's a picture floating around social media land that says, "Men, if you ever want to know what a woman's mind feels like, imagine a browser with 2,857 tabs open. All. The. Time."

Right?

Then there are the actual activities happening simultaneously. I can be folding laundry, giving a math test, cooking dinner, and planning our family vacation all at once. My husband can't handle more than one subject. When we are talking and I go off on a rabbit trail (that makes perfect sense to me, by the way), his mind hangs there until I get back to the original subject and he never heard all the off-topic things I said.

Years ago we were having a Fourth of July party with five other families coming for hot dogs and s'mores, followed by a family fireworks display. I asked him to run and pick out whatever fireworks he wanted and requested he take our four-year-old with him because she was underfoot and keeping me from getting the dessert made.

He hesitantly agreed, not because he minds having the kids with him, but because he gets overloaded with excitement at the fireworks stand and didn't know if he could pay enough attention to what he was spending if he had an active four-year-old along.

I gave him that look. You know the one. It says, "Really? I am laying fruit out in the shape of the American flag while nursing a baby and supervising three children cleaning all the bathrooms … and you can't take one stinkin' four-year-old to the fireworks stand?"

He took her with him.

When he got home forty-five minutes later, the guests were arriving and the party was getting started. I headed outside with a platter of buns and bowls of chips and started entertaining. We were having a terrific time when I asked him, "Hey, hon, where's the four-year-old?" We looked around and she was nowhere to be found. I started to panic and our guests all stopped to help us look, and finally, just as I was about to call out the fireman and police and any other authority I could think of, she was found sleeping in the back of my husband's car.

He had gotten home and, in the excitement, had forgotten she was back there.

Yes, she was fine, and yes, nothing happened to her and she never even knew she was missing. But *I. was. a. basket. case.*

I thought it was a huge deal, and all the other women at the party agreed. My husband thought it was no big deal at all, and all the men agreed.

Men and women are just different; we all know that. But it's sixteen years later and I still get heart palpitations when I think of that day.

I, like all women, am a complicated creature. Not only can I do a dozen things at once, but I can be crying one minute and laughing the next. We are brilliantly capable and wonderfully made. Men are too, by the way, just in different, vital ways.

This chapter is about many of the little things we do—things that might go unnoticed or seem unimportant. Everyday activities such as cooking and shopping that don't need a whole chapter but do take up time and energy and need to be balanced.

Some of these will overlap with some of the previous chapters in ways, but they are unique in their challenges. Some areas will fall into money *and* home. Or motherhood *and* moods. We are not simple creatures, and our lives aren't on a single track at any point.

SHOP 'TIL YOU DROP

One thing we all have to do, like it or not, is shop. Personally, I like shopping. But I know a lot of women who hate it (I don't understand them, but I love them!). Shopping affects my finances, my marriage, my time away from my family, and how I take care of my home.

This can get out of balance very, very easily. You may find that you are running to the grocery store every day or maybe you are escaping to the mall and need to stop. Do you buy things you don't need? (Guilty!) Do you shop without a budget?

Using the BALANCE plan, you can get this back into balance with some easy steps:

1. Make a schedule for your shopping needs and stick to it. If you forgot something, then do without it. Having to figure that out a few times will teach you to be careful to get what you need.

2. Keep a running list. In our kitchen we have a chalkboard where anyone can write down anything they need. Also, if someone uses the last of something, they should write it there. That way I don't suddenly realize I am out of detergent or sugar. I can check the list.

3. Share shopping with a friend. I like Costco; my friend likes Sam's. So when I need a Sam's item she picks it up for me, and I do the same for her at Costco. If your neighbor goes to the grocery store every Friday, then maybe she can pick up something for you. Just remember to either have cash on hand or be able to Paypal the money right away. Owing a friend gets complicated!

4. Have a budget and stick to it. We talked about this in the "Money Matters" chapter, but in reference to shopping, know how much you have to spend before you leave the house, and don't let yourself go beyond that.

5. Have a free day. Being someone who likes to shop, once a month I have a free shopping day that's not designated for groceries or buying necessities. I can go around to the stores I have been wanting to stop in and get some small shopping done. I still have a budget, but my time is open.

6. Beware of online shopping tricks. I love to shop online since my small town doesn't have many stores with what I need. But I have to set a limit before I go look online or I will get caught in the web of "If you add ten dollars, we will send you a free_____" or "Other people who bought that also bought this!" I can just feel the end of the sentence that's missing: "You sucker!"

Uncontrolled shopping can end marriages and break families. It fills our homes with junk we don't need and empties our lives of things that have real value.

HOLIDAYS AREN'T ALWAYS WHAT WE EXPECT

Shopping is only one of the issues we deal with when it comes to holidays. Extended family, parties, and finding time to wrap gifts, decorate trees, and put lights on the house—it's all a chore, yet it's supposed to be fun.

Holidays get out of balance more quickly in this society of extravagance and extremity. Sit down before the holiday gets going and make some plans for staying in balance. I know Christmas creeps up quickly, but we do know it's coming. Make a reasonable budget, eliminate a few things, ask the kids what they would like, and work on a schedule.

Don't cram your schedule so much that you don't enjoy the time together. If you're doing all of the cooking for Thanksgiving, why not enlist help or buy a few side dishes premade? Some of you may balk at that, and I admit that I am not a great cook; but I also know that if I can save a few hours in prep time, then I am a better hostess.

Here are a few ideas for keeping holidays in balance:

1. Like I said before and will probably say again, have a budget. While you're penciling in your activities, write in a few days of "doing nothing." Your family needs a break.

2. For special occasions that are specific to your family, like birthdays and anniversaries, don't compare yourself to others. Just because the lady down the street had pony rides and a bounce house at her three-year-old's party doesn't mean you have to keep up with that. Do what fits your family's style and budget.

3. Picnics are the best! For those three-day weekends all year, get together with friends and have a picnic

or barbeque. If you don't know who to invite, just brainstorm and do it. It doesn't have to be perfect or Pinterest worthy. Release yourself from thinking you can't invite people over until your house is perfect or you know how to make kabob. Just plop some dogs on a stick and roast 'em.

4. Look for ways to do free things! Valentine's Day is a favorite around here. I will buy a little bit of candy and then write love notes to each child (and of course my husband!) and give them coupons for special things we can do together. The coupons are for a dance, a listening ear, a drive, dessert alone, playing a game, and so on. They can use their coupons anytime they want, no questions asked, and I will stop anything (within reason) to honor it on the spot.

Use holidays as opportunities to narrow in on what's important, and remember what the Bible says about putting anything before Him. This can also be an amazing time of mending bruised relationships by giving gifts from the heart like apologies and forgiveness.

IT'S SCHOOL TIME

Whether you homeschool or your kids go to a school, you will have challenges with an education system. This is motherhood, ministry, money, mates, and sometimes even mouth and moods!

This vital element of your child's life causes us to have to go so far out of our comfort zones that we may as well change our zip codes.

As a homeschooler, I have to wake up every morning with the confidence that I am going to be able to drill information into my child's head today and not ruin him in the process. For those who leave home for school, you are dealing with regulations and other people's schedules and many obstacles that keep you from knowing for sure what your child needs during the day. Neither one is easy to balance!

Things that can get easily out of balance with school issues are time management, pressure from others, lack of understanding, fatigue, and frustration. I encourage you to take each problem you're having with school and give it to God. He has answers for you and solutions you would never have thought of on your own.

Many, many times I have been at the end of my rope with a child in school. I did not know how I was going to get through to them or what to do when they flunked. So I prayed and prayed and kept moving ahead. And God has always come through. Either I will get a divine idea, or the child will have a break-through, or my husband will offer to step in, or a phone call out of the blue will offer solutions.

Be patient with yourself and remember that school is thirteen years plus. You don't have to solve everything right now. And if you see some trouble ahead, God has that in His hands too and He knows exactly what to do. You do what you should and no more. Leave the rest to Him.

LET ME ENTERTAIN YOU

My last miscellaneous topic is a biggie these day: entertainment. Movies, TV, books, video games, Wii, YouTube—so many ways now to stop and entertain ourselves. It is a trap and we have got to be intentional if we are going to stay out of it.

I can be doing great about not watching too much TV or overchecking Instagram, then before I know it, I have wasted two hours. It's so mindless and relaxing that we get lost in it and it is a *time sucker.*

Look, I watch TV, I like movies, and I love a good IG photo, but I know if I don't give myself some serious limits, I will fall prey to the spirit of "leave me alone, kids, I'm watching something." I know this sounds harsh, but if you are doing too much of any of these things, I would encourage you to take a complete break from it all for a few weeks. It's like hitting the reset button. You need to remember what you've been missing. For me, when I get out of balance in the area of entertainment, I make myself go cold turkey until I'm not thinking about it anymore.

It does consume our thoughts regardless if we want to admit it. The Bible is clear: "Finally, brothers, whatever is true, whatever is honorable, whatever is just, whatever is pure, whatever is lovely, whatever is commendable, if there is any excellence, if there is anything worthy of praise, think about these things" (Phil. 4:8). Yikes! Them's some pretty strong standards!

The trap of entertaining ourselves is one that we all fall into, some more than others. You have to decide for yourself how much is too much. Don't let yourself justify too much by telling yourself you deserve it or that it's less than your husband does or that you need it to unwind. Be honest and guarded about how much you are doing simply for empty, or even harmful, pleasure.

There are many more areas that fall between the previous chapters. I really want you to know that everything that is important to you is important to God. He cares about your small battles as much as the huge ones. You are a precious woman who gets out of balance sometimes like all other women of the world. He wants to help you find your way.

ASSIGNMENT

Find a song that inspires you to make positive changes in your life, be yourself, and embrace life. Now, play that song at least once a day, and if you're so inspired, dance around to it!

13

MAKING IT WORK

Have I not commanded you? Be strong and courageous.
Do not be frightened, and do not be dismayed, for the
LORD *your God is with you wherever you go.*

Joshua 1:9

A writer's life is not as glamorous as you might think. In fact, just moments ago as I was typing, I had two little boys knocking on my door telling me they have an important question to ask me. So I gave them permission to come in, and they asked me, "Is there a roller coaster at Epcot?"

I spend some whole days in my pajamas and I eat whatever's leftover for lunch even if it's a reheated corn-dog reject from lunch the day before. I have no pride when it comes to finding food. I don't have the time while book writing to make myself a fine plate of photographable food.

My life, when I am facing a deadline, is out of balance. I am not showering as much as I really should, I don't pay enough attention to my kids, and my husband is the last person on my list because, frankly, he can take care of himself right now.

And you know what? It's all okay. This is part of my life and I also know there will be a time when I can take a month off and just give my family mucho quality time. I will be able to shower and do laundry and eat veggies. It's part of that "there's a time for everything" verse. Right now is my time to write.

I tell you this because I don't want you to think that just because your life is not a beautifully balanced masterpiece of perfection that anything is wrong. Sometimes we just need to focus on one or two things. As long as we don't stay there for too long, it is completely fine.

The difference between this kind of imbalance and the kind you need to correct ASAP is that I planned this. I knew I would need writing time, and I set aside the free time in the future to balance it out. But when you are not controlling it or planning it and it's not what you really want or who you desire to be, then you need to make changes. Or if you are in a crisis situation, like a medical issue that takes all of your attention, it's necessary.

Being intentional is the word for today. Plan it, embrace it, enjoy it.

Avoid getting caught up in rules that aren't real. We impose our own ideas on ourselves and one another and not enough of God's ideas. That's part of why I put so much focus on learning God's Word and burying it in your heart and mind. The more you do that, the closer you will be to finding true balance in all areas.

We try to tell ourselves that we should be based on outside influences, like what we see on TV or online. Someone says all women should be thin and we believe it. We see the magazine pics of someone's home and feel like we are doing it all wrong. But those are rules we put on ourselves; they are not true. You are doing something someone else can't, and they are doing some things that you can't. Be yourself and let God use you.

I WANT A FEAST!

We want it all and we want no waiting or inconveniences. We want the front of the line, a discount price, and special consideration. That's the way of the brat. I don't want to be a brat; I just want my way.

Problems, lack, mistakes, mistreatment, and injustice will always be happening somewhere in your life. If you didn't cause it, then someone else's bumbling or selfishness probably did. Okay, big deal. Should you never suffer? It's not the fact that you have problems that you need to work on; it's how you respond to them that matters.

A well-balanced life is not free of troubles. In fact, those troubles give us strength for the next issue that arises. If we are avoiding any pain or upset, then we are robbing ourselves of the real joy of pulling ourselves up again and the lessons we will learn.

I have given you several assignments involving something to do first thing in the morning. That's because starting your day off with a good handle on your vision wrapped up in God's love is the best way to begin your journey to balance.

I HAVE TOO MANY IMBALANCES!

Some of you might be feeling overwhelmed because you have a problem in every area. Your personal health is poor, your marriage is suffering, your kids have gone wild, and let's not even discuss the bank account. If this is you, don't give up; you can make changes. Choose a place to begin, just one for now. Then slowly add as you see changes.

What you will discover is that when you correct one area, the others begin to change on their own. If you're eating out less because you want to take better care of yourself, your finances will reflect that. When your marriage gets stronger, your kids will see a change and naturally respond. It's not a guarantee, but it is certain that when one member of a family makes changes for the better, the rest of the family is affected.

Don't believe the lies that your mind wants to whisper to you that say you can't change: "People don't change," "I was born this way," "I am not strong enough." We were all born with weaknesses and we may always have a struggle with something, but you can make better choices and overcome. You can find joy and peace and balance in your current situation.

When you get started and see some benefits and begin to feel even more strength build, you may have a setback. You might gain a few pounds or have a moment of weakness or let your mouth fly off the handle. Do *not* let that tell you that you've failed. It's just more lessons and more opportunities.

When my son does his math and he gets a problem wrong, I tell him, "Try this one again." Then he will occasionally get it wrong the second time. Is he a math failure? Of course not! He just needs to learn how to do it. So we work together, I keep giving him problems until eventually he gets it, and we move on to the next concept. If we just said, "Okay, you can't do it so forget it; just stay the way you are," he would never be able to move ahead and do more complicated math. He needs that for his future.

I know you don't want to wait. You want the changes to happen now. But you have things to learn, and I am telling you, if you will trust God with the lessons, you will become the kind of woman that you would greatly admire. It is through suffering and effort that we become beautiful.

NOW WHAT?

We are at the end of our conversation, and it's now in your hands to find the kind of balance you want. I know you can; I believe in you. And even better, I believe in a God who picks up your slack and covers all of your weaknesses.

I will probably still fall down occasionally; I think it's part of my calling! I have literally fallen down in many places: movie theaters, escalators, grocery stores, getting on a boat (I'll tell you that story sometime!). It's embarrassing to fall. And I'm not young anymore. I don't just pop back up and keep walking like a toddler does. But I always learn something from those falls. And now I'm smarter because of those lessons.

I am expecting great things from you. Close your eyes and picture the woman you want to be, that you believe you can be, in five years. Now, go become her.

ACKNOWLEDGMENTS

This book is a product of so many people supporting me and believing in the project that I have to give a few special mentions.

To my husband, James, you bless me with your patience. You've let me disappear to write and cry on your shoulder when I didn't know if I could get it done. You amaze me every day with your willingness to put up with my falls and messes. And a special thanks for letting me tell all of our silly stories to the world.

To my kids, Grace, Jacob, Hope, Faith, Patience, Noah, Adam, Elijah, and Levi ... how could I breathe without you? You have waited so patiently for me to emerge from my writing cave to talk to me. You always ask me how it's going before you ask me what's for dinner. You're brilliant and beautiful and bold, and I am so thankful that God let me be your mom!

To my girlfriends Sara and Sharra and Pennie, who have stuck by me while I write, thank you for dragging me out to dinner so often and making me laugh so hard that I forget my struggles. Thank you for listening to my pity parties and telling me to just get over it in your loving way. You are each a huge part of this book. I can't imagine doing life without you.

To my agent, Don Jacobson, you believed in me when I was just a Texas mom pounding away on the keyboard. Your support has meant more than I could ever express, and I thank God for putting us together in such a weird and wacky way. You've become a friend, and for that I am so, so grateful.

To my peeps at David C Cook, Ingrid, Darren, and Lisa B., thank you a million times for sticking with me through this effort and putting up with my trillion questions. You all are rock stars!

To Nicci, my editor extraordinaire, boy, oh boy, you had your work cut out for you with me. Thank you for your brilliance, thank you for your patience, thank you for making this book a thousand times better.

To the blog readers who have stuck so faithfully with me through life's journeys, you all are my scarecrow … you bless me most of all. We've been through thick and thin together, and you're always cheering me on and sending me notes of encouragement. You make me smile every day.

And thanks forever to my sweet Savior, Jesus Christ, who died for me and teaches me daily to die to self.

I can't say thanks enough to each of you, so I carry you with me and hope you know how amazing you are!

NOTES

CHAPTER 1: BALANCE: WHAT IS IT?

1. Shauna Niequist, *Bittersweet: Thoughts on Change, Grace, and Learning the Hard Way* (Grand Rapids, MI: Zondervan), 233.

2. John Maxwell, *Learning from the Giants: Life and Leadership Lessons from the Bible* (New York: FaithWords, 2002), 53.

CHAPTER 2: SPELLING IT OUT

1. Kristen Strong, *Girl Meets Change: Truths to Carry You through Life's Transitions* (Grand Rapids, MI: Revell, 2015), 172.

2. John MacArthur, *Found: God's Peace: Experience True Freedom from Anxiety in Every Circumstance* (Colorado Springs: David C Cook, 2015), 47–48.

CHAPTER 3: ME, MYSELF, AND I

1. Wayne Jacobsen, *He Loves Me!: Learning to Live in the Father's Affection*, 2nd ed. (Newbury Park, CA: Windblown Media, 2007), 141.

2. John Dunlop, *Wellness for the Glory of God: Living Well after Forty with Joy and Contentment in All of Life* (Wheaton, IL: Crossway, 2014), 32.

3. Lysa TerKeurst, *Made to Crave: Satisfying Your Deepest Desire with God, Not Food* (Grand Rapids, MI: Zondervan, 2010), 93.

4. Emily P. Freeman, *Grace for the Good Girl: Letting Go of the Try-Hard Life* (Grand Rapids, MI: Revell, 2011), 20.

CHAPTER 4: BEING MARRIED

1. Gary Thomas, *Sacred Marriage: What If God Designed Marriage to Make Us Holy More Than to Make Us Happy?* (Grand Rapids, MI: Zondervan, 2000), 13.

2. Henry Cloud and John Townsend, *Boundaries in Marriage: Understanding the Choices That Make or Break Loving Relationships* (Grand Rapids, MI: Zondervan, 1999), 44.

3. Thomas, *Sacred Marriage*, 212.

4. Melanie Shankle, *The Antelope in the Living Room: The Real Story of Two People Sharing One Life* (Carol Stream, IL: Tyndale, 2014), xv.

CHAPTER 5: MOTHERHOOD

1. Lysa TerKeurst, *Am I Messing Up My Kids? And Other Questions Every Mom Asks* (Eugene, OR: Harvest, 2006), 131–32.

2. John Rosemond, *Parenting by the Book: Biblical Wisdom for Raising Your Child* (New York: Howard Books, 2007), 153.

3. Patrick M. Quinn and Ken Roach, *How to Ruin Your Child in Seven Easy Steps: Tame Your Vices, Nurture Their Virtues* (Colorado Springs: David C Cook, 2015), 175.

4. Quinn and Roach, *How to Ruin*, 23.

CHAPTER 6: HOME SWEET HOME

1. Myquillyn Smith, *The Nesting Place: It Doesn't Have to Be Perfect to Be Beautiful* (Grand Rapids, MI: Zondervan, 2014), 185.

2. Crystal Paine, *Say Goodbye to Survival Mode: Nine Simple Strategies to Stress Less, Sleep More, and Restore Your Passion for Life* (Nashville: Nelson Books, 2014), 143.

3. Barbara Reich, *Secrets of an Organized Mom: From the Overflowing Closets to the Chaotic Play Areas: A Room-by-Room Guide to Decluttering and Streamlining Your Home for a Happier Family* (New York: Atria, 2013), 237.

CHAPTER 7: GETTING OUT OF THE HOUSE

1. Greg McKeown, *Essentialism: The Disciplined Pursuit of Less* (New York: Crown Business, 2014), 7.

2. McKeown, *Essentialism*, 85.

3. Henry Cloud and John Townsend, *Boundaries: When to Say Yes, How to Say No to Take Control of Your Life* (Grand Rapids, MI: Zondervan, 1992), 109.

4. John Maxwell, *Wisdom from Women of the Bible: Giants of the Faith Speak into Our Lives* (New York: FaithWords, 2015), 89–90.

5. Lysa TerKeurst, *The Best Yes: Making Wise Decisions in the Midst of Endless Demands* (Nashville: Nelson Books, 2014), 165.

CHAPTER 8: THE BLESSING OF FRIENDS

1. C. S. Lewis, *The Four Loves* (Boston: Mariner Books, 2012), 8.

2. Candace Cameron Bure, *Balancing It All: My Story of Juggling Priorities and Purpose* (Nashville: B&H, 2014), 64.

3. Anne Graham Lotz, *Wounded by God's People: Discovering How God's Love Heals Our Hearts* (London: Hodder & Stoughton, 2013), 212.

4. John Townsend, *Beyond Boundaries: Learning to Trust Again in Relationships* (Grand Rapids, MI: Zondervan, 2011), 126–27.

5. C. S. Lewis, *Mere Christianity* (New York: HarperOne, 2001), 131.

CHAPTER 9: MONEY MATTERS

1. David Ramsey, *The Legacy Journey: A Radical View of Biblical Wealth and Generosity* (Brentwood, TN: Ramsey Press, 2014), 55.

2. Ramsey, *Legacy Journey*, 225.

CHAPTER 10: TAMING THE TONGUE

1. James MacDonald, *Lord, Change My Attitude: Before It's Too Late* (Chicago: Moody, 2008), 131.

2. Karen Ehman, *Keep It Shut: What to Say, How to Say It, and When to Say Nothing at All* (Grand Rapids, MI: Zondervan, 2015), 127.

3. Ehman, *Keep It Shut*, 180.

CHAPTER 11: MOODS: YEP, I'M GOING THERE

1. Gary Chapman, *Anger: Handling a Powerful Emotion in a Healthy Way* (Chicago: Northfield Press, 2007), 57.

2. Lysa TerKeurst, *Unglued: Making Wise Choices in the Midst of Raw Emotions* (Grand Rapids, MI: Zondervan, 2012), 16.

3. TerKeurst, *Unglued*, 72.

FOR MOMS IN THE TRENCHES!

How do you stop and start over when you're exhausted, the kids aren't cooperating, and annoyance is getting the best of you? Lisa Pennington shares her personal story of embracing contentment and shows you fun and practical ways to "reset" when you're in the trenches of a difficult mothering day.

Lisa Pennington is a homeschooling mother of nine who shares her life—one laundry load at a time—on her popular blog called *The Pennington Point*.

Available in print and digital editions everywhere books are sold

transforming lives together